REMEMBERING THE 75TH ANNIVERSARY OF THE KOREAN WAR

THE STORY OF UN KOREAN WAR VETERANS

Edited by Ha Young Shin | Associate Editor Jihae Yun | Supervision Hosub Shim

HISTORY LIVES IN EVERY PAGE...

16 COUNTRIES!

도서출판 코레드

THE STORY OF
UN KOREAN WAR VETERANS

HISTORY LIVES IN
EVERY PAGE...

16
COUNTRIES!

Foreword

The Freedom They Defended, The Legacy We Carry

On the 75th anniversary of the outbreak of the Korean War, we are reminded once more of a generation whose courage shaped the course of history. In 1950, when war broke out on the Korean Peninsula, young men from across the world responded—not for conquest or gain, but for a cause greater than themselves: the defense of freedom in a land most had never known.

Under the banner of the United Nations, soldiers from 16 nations came to Korea's aid. They stood shoulder to shoulder in the face of tyranny, answering the call not of empire, but of humanity. It was one of the earliest and most enduring demonstrations of international solidarity in the name of peace and democratic values.

They came as strangers. Many would never return home. Yet their legacy lives on—not only in the democratic and prosperous nation that South Korea has become, but also in the hearts of their children and grandchildren who continue to remember and honor their sacrifice.

This book is a sacred collection of those memories. Through the voices of the descendants of Korean War veterans, we hear not just the echoes of war, but the

Annie Chan
President, Korea-U.S. Alliance USA (KUAUF)

enduring love and pride of families who carry forward a legacy of valor. Each story is a living testament to the price of liberty and to the power of remembrance.

Freedom is never free. It must be protected, sustained, and passed on. The families who contributed to this book understand that truth deeply. Their reflections are not only personal tributes, but also collective acknowledgments that the sacrifices made over seven decades ago still matter—profoundly and urgently.

As we turn the pages of this volume, may we do so with gratitude and reverence. May we remember that today's Korea stands not by chance, but by the blood and devotion of those who fought for its future. And may we renew our commitment to ensuring that such sacrifices are never forgotten.

Preserving freedom through strength— this enduring truth remains the foundation of peace. The strength of character, the strength of conviction, and the strength of alliance are what preserved liberty then and what must preserve it now.

To all who served, and to their families who continue to bear the torch of memory and honor: we thank you. This book is for you.

Preface

The Echo of Noble Valor and Devotion

We must remember, the freedom and peace we enjoy today were not given by chance. They were made possible by the noble courage and devotion of the UN forces who fought alongside us under the sacred cause of freedom, when the fate of the Republic of Korea hung by a thread 75 years ago, at dawn on June 25, 1950, due to North Korea's sudden invasion.

This book was written with a heartfelt desire to help future generations truly understand the immense bravery and sacrifice of the UN veterans, whose stories risk being forgotten with time. Through this remembrance, we hope to build a lasting bond with their descendants and renew our shared commitment to protecting global peace and security for generations to come.

To promote greater awareness and appreciation, KAFSP[1] invited 70 descendants of UN veterans to the KMA [Korea Military Academy] on November 3, 2023, to participate in an event aimed at fostering empathy, promoting the importance of veterans, and strengthening ties with participating nations. During the event, attendees observed the cadets' guard of honor ceremony and enjoyed performances by students from SDC School. The descendants unanimously expressed, "We had a truly meaningful time. Please hold this event regularly every year." and supported making it an annual tradition.

---

1) KAFSP(Center for Korea-America Freedom & Security Policy)
   Objectives of the organization : Support to strengthening the ROK-US alliance and establishing stong national security posture

A group photo of participants

KMA cadets' guard of honor ceremony

On February 27, 2024, KAFSP established Y-KAFSP at its office with the participation of approximately 30 descendants of UN veterans, creating a dedicated space for dialogue. Ilayda Asimgil, a student at Hankuk University of Foreign Studies, was appointed as the representative of Y-KAFSP, and regular meetings were planned.

On May 26, 2024, as part of activities to better understand Korea, a trip to the Gangneung area on the East Coast was organized. 40 descendants of UN veterans participated, visiting Ojukheon, a well-known cultural site, and enjoying the beautiful scenery of Korea's East Sea. During a casual conversation, the idea of publishing a book titled "The Story of My Grandfather, a UN Veteran" was brought up.

February 27, 2024 Y-KAFSP

May 26, 2024 Gangneung Tour

On October 24, 2024, the second Invitational Event to the KMA for International Students from UN Participating Nations was held. Approximately 80 university students who are descendants of UN veterans and 30 Korean university students visited the KMA together. They watched the KMA cadets' Hwarang Ceremony and participated in a presentation session of "The Story of My Grandfather, a UN Veteran."

During the presentation session, Ms. Stephanie, a student from Sookmyung Women's University, shared, "My grandfather, Santiago Gaona, was the youngest Colombian soldier to join the Korean War. He was only 16 years old when he arrived in June 1951, after sailing for 30 days to reach Korea. In August 1952, during a night patrol, his vehicle was attacked with enemy grenades. He was injured in the attack and returned home in December 1952." The attendees unanimously agreed on the importance of publishing such valuable lessons in a book to pass them on to the younger generation.

A group photo of participants

A group photo with KMA cadets

Finally, on February 1, 2025, during a Y-KAFSP meeting, it was decided to publish the book "The Story of Korean War UN Veterans," with plans to release it in June to commemorate and remember the outbreak of the Korean War on June 25, 1950. Due to the challenge of locating descendants from 16 UN participating nations currently residing in Korea, out of the 22 manuscript submissions, 10 were submitted by international students in Korea and 12 by descendants living abroad.

Sincere gratitude is extended to Professor Hosub Shim of the Department of Military History at Korea Military Academy and Ms. Jihae Yun, a student at the University of Toronto, for their devoted efforts in the publication of this book.

Ha Young Shin
Editor-in-chief

Index

Foreword — 004
Preface — 006

Part 1 Overview of the Korean War

Background and the Causes of the Outbreak of the Korean War — 014
Phases of the Korean War, 1950–1953 — 018
UN Forces' Participation in the Korean War — 020

Part 2 The Legacy of the Korean War Veterans

UNITED STATES
Those Who Answered the Call to Defend People They Never Met — *Aidan Fleer* — 025
Two War Hero — *Alexander Pratt* — 033

UNITED KINGDOM
Our Hero — *Carly Bidwell* — 041

AUSTRALIA
Across the Water: Remembering My Great Uncle — *Oliver Healy* — 051

NETHERLANDS
The Story of My Father, Korean War Veteran Colonel Leendert Schreuders — *Leo Schreuders* — 059

CANADA
Bridging Generations: A Canadian Veteran's Story and Korea's Lasting Honor — *Rachel Cote* — 069

NEW ZEALAND
Echoes of Courage: My Grandfather's Legacy in the Korean War — *Keishon R. Lynch* — 077

THAILAND
Inheritance of Honor: Memories and Values from My Grandfather's Service — *Wasita Sritragool* — 087

GREECE
The Story of my Grandfather; a Korean War Veteran — *Socrates Boutsikaris* — 095

SOUTH AFRICA
Alexis "Topper" van der Spuy: My Grandfather, My Hero, and a Hero of the Korean War — *Alessia Stefanutti* — 101

BELGIUM
The Story of my Father, Korean War Veteran Gustave Michel Sourbron — *Lilianne Sourbron* — 109

PHILIPPINES
A Legacy of Kapwa between the Philippines and Korea — *Mary Ellen Burro* — 119
Continuing the Legacy: Writing the Next Chapter of the Story — *Joon Shin Encomienda Amangan* — 126

TÜRKIYE
My Grandfather's Past, My Future with Republic of Korea — *Ilayda Asımgil* — 137
A Stone of Memory, A Pillar of Friendship: The Story of Ahmet Şahna, "Koreli Ahmet" — *Eren Yıldırım* — 144

LUXEMBOURG
The Diary-Writing Soldier, Jean Stoffel — *Max Stoffel* — 155

COLOMBIA
From Cali to Seoul: Carrying My Grandfather's Legacy — *Stephanie Arguello Gaona* — 163
A Step Forward — *Valentina Rojas Martinez* — 172

ETHIOPIA
Echoes of Honor: The Legacy of Korean War Veterans and Their Descendants' Journey — *Wakjira Gemechu* — 181
Echoes of Sacrifice: An Ethiopian Soldier's Journey and the Future We Must Build — *Bethelehem Solomon Shenkute* — 191

FRANCE
Silent Hero: My Grandfather, a French Veteran in the Korean War — *Alice Prigl d'Ondel* — 203

USA / REPUBLIC OF KOREA
A Forgotten Fighter from a Forgotten Unit in a Forgotten War — *Monika Choi Stoy* — 211

WE REMEMBER — 221

Part 3 Echoes of Gratitude from Korea

The Land Your Grandfather Visited — *Yoon Ha* — 224
In the Names of Heroes — *Ph.D Hyuk Chul Kwon* — 228
A Letter written in Love — *Minsub Kim* — 232
Letter of Gratitude — *Jion Mun* — 234
Ending Note — *Jihae Yun* — 236

Part 1
Overview of the Korean War

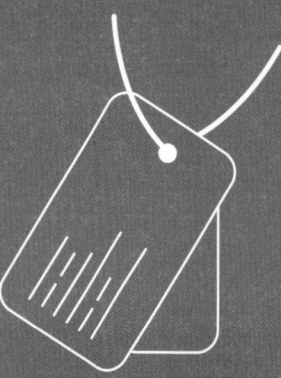

Overview of the Korean War
Background and the Causes of the Outbreak of the Korean War
Phases of the Korean War, 1950 –1953
UN Forces' Participation in the Korean War

Background and the Causes of the Outbreak of the Korean War

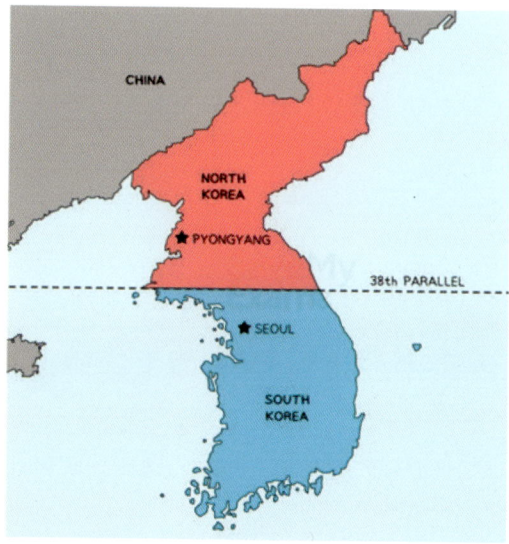

A map showing how Korea was divided in 1945

With the defeat of the Japanese Empire on August 15, 1945, the Korean Peninsula was liberated from Japanese colonial rule. After liberation, compatriots who had been fighting for independence returned one after another, and everyone dreamed of establishing a new democratic republic, inheriting 5,000 years of history. However, in December 1945, the victorious powers of World War II— the United States, the United Kingdom, and the Soviet Union— decided at the Moscow Conference of Foreign Ministers to implement a five-year trusteeship over Korea and to establish a provisional government. This was intended to prevent the chaos that might arise from the sudden establishment of an independent government.

However, a trusteeship was not what we, who had the capacity for self-governance, wanted. The bigger problem was the tacit agreement between the United States and the

Soviet Union to divide and occupy the Korean Peninsula along the 38th parallel and to implement a military government.

Thus, the U.S. forces were stationed south of the 38th parallel, and the Soviet forces in the north. Subsequently, the U.S. and the Soviet Union implemented military governments and convened the U.S.-Soviet Joint Commission (1946-1947) to seek the establishment of a unified Korean government. However, unlike the United States, which sought to establish a unified government for the entire Korean Peninsula, the Soviet Union had a strategic intention to establish a communist regime in the north and solidify the division.

Ultimately, the two sides could not narrow their differences over the composition of a provisional government, and the Joint Commission failed. The United States then referred the issue to the United Nations. In November 1947, the UN General Assembly resolved to hold general elections under UN supervision throughout Korea to establish a unified government. In January 1948, the United Nations Temporary Commission on Korea (UNTCOK) arrived in Seoul to support the elections. However, the Soviet Union, which wanted to keep at least the north within its sphere of influence, refused simultaneous elections in both the north and south. As a result, in February 1948, the UN decided to hold elections only in areas where it was possible under its supervision, that is, only in the south. [Accordingly, general elections were held only in South Korea on May 10, 1948, and on August 15, 1948, the government of the Republic of Korea was finally established.]

On December 12, 1948, the UN General Assembly officially recognized the Republic of Korea as the "only legitimate government in Korea" by an overwhelming margin: 48 in favor, 6 against, and 1 abstention. North Korea, which had refused to participate in the nationwide elections, established the "Democratic People's Republic of Korea" on September 9 of that year. Thus began the history of division, with the Republic of Korea representing the free world in the south and the Democratic People's Republic of Korea representing the communist bloc in the north.

With the establishment of two separate governments on the Korean Peninsula in 1948, the Soviet and the U.S. forces, who had supported military government formation, withdrew, leaving behind only military advisory missions. After the withdrawal of both countries' forces, the Republic of Korea devoted itself to political, economic, and social development. However, Kim Il-sung of North Korea was different. He dreamed of becoming the sole leader of the entire peninsula through armed unification. For this purpose, he strengthened his military with powerful Soviet tanks and equipment, supported by the Soviet Union and China.

By 1950, North Korea had completed its war preparations and possessed overwhelming military power compared to the South, constantly seeking an opportunity to invade.

Then, on January 12, 1950, the Acheson Line, declared by Dean Acheson (1893-1971), the U.S. Secretary of State, changed the course of East Asian history. The Acheson Line included the Japanese archipelago and the Philippines, but excluded the Korean Peninsula. From a military standpoint, the Acheson Line implied that the U.S. military would not actively intervene in the event of an emergency on the Korean Peninsula.

Kim Il-sung misinterpreted this as a weakening of America's will to defend South Korea and saw it as a golden opportunity to invade. Confident of victory, he explained his invasion plan to Stalin of the Soviet Union and Mao Zedong of China and obtained their approval. Stalin and Mao, seeing little likelihood of U.S. intervention, approved the invasion, and promised military support, aiming to secure leadership within the communist bloc and expand communism in Northeast Asia.

At dawn on Sunday, June 25, 1950, North Korea launched its invasion with the ambition of communist unification.

Phases of the Korean War, 1950–1953

❶ North Korea's Surprise Attack and Retreat to the Nakdong River Line
(June 25 – September 14, 1950)

- The South Korean military lost Seoul in just three days. (June 28)
- U.N. forces joined the war. (July 1)
- Allied forces retreated to the Nakdong River Line. (June 25 – July 31)
- The Nakdong River defense line was fiercely defended. (August 1 – September 14)

❷ Incheon Landing Operation and Advance to the Yalu River
(September 15 – October 24, 1950)

- The Incheon Landing Operation succeeded. (September 15)
- After a counterattack on the Nakdong River front, ROK and U.N. forces retook Seoul (September 28) and recovered the 38th parallel. (September 30)
- After crossing the 38th parallel on October 1, ROK and U.N. forces advanced to Chosan, near the Yalu River. (October 1 – October 26)

❸ Chinese Intervention and Renewed Warfare (October 25, 1950 – July 9, 1951)

- By October 25, over 250,000 Chinese troops had crossed the Yalu River, preparing for a surprise attack on the Korean and U.N. forces. These attacks occurred five times until May the following year.
- ROK and UN. forces abandoned Seoul again a month after retreating from Pyongyang. (December 4)
- Eventually, they retreated to the 37th parallel, between Pyeongtaek and Samcheok. After retaking Seoul (March 15), the battle around the 38th parallel resumed.

❹ Ceasefire Negotiations and the Battle for High Ground (July 10, 1951 – July 27, 1953)

- On July 10, 1951, the UN. and communist forces began ceasefire negotiations. However, throughout the two-year-long negotiations, fierce battles continued over control of high ground and territory.

An armistice agreement was signed at Panmunjom by North Korea, China, and the United Nations Command. South Korea did not sign the agreement, meaning that, technically, the two Koreas are still at war. They remain divided along the Military Demarcation Line, which was established in 1953.

UN Forces' Participation in the Korean War

After World War II, the international community sought to establish a collective security system to preserve global peace and stability. As part of this effort, the United Nations (UN) was founded on October 24, 1945, with 51 member states. According to Article 1 of the UN Charter, its primary purpose was to maintain international peace and security. This commitment was put to the test with the outbreak of the Korean War in 1950, marking the first large-scale deployment of UN forces in history.

When North Korea invaded South Korea on June 25, 1950, the UN immediately recognized the international implications of the conflict. The UN Security Council convened an emergency meeting on the same day and passed Resolution 82, calling for an immediate cessation of hostilities, the withdrawal of North Korean troops to the 38th parallel, and adherence to the principles of the UN Charter. North Korea, however, ignored this resolution and continued its offensive.

In response, the United States proposed a new resolution. On June 27, the Security Council adopted Resolution 83, authorizing member states to provide military assistance to South Korea in order to repel the armed aggression and restore peace in the region. This marked the first instance of the UN invoking collective security measures to address a breach of international peace.

The Security Council on June 27, 1950

To coordinate the multinational response, the UN Secretary-General recommended the establishment of a unified command. On July 7, the Security Council passed Resolution 84, officially creating the UN Command and designating the United States to lead it. This resolution called upon all contributing nations to place their forces under the unified command. On July 8, the U.S. President Harry Truman appointed General Douglas MacArthur, then Commander of the U.S. Far East Command, as Commander-in-Chief of the UN Forces. Operational control over South Korean troops was transferred to the UN on July 14, with Lieutenant General Walton Walker of the Eighth U.S. Army taking charge of ground operations.

MacArthur's military strategy was to delay the North Korean advance in the south, weaken their offensive capabilities, and prepare a counteroffensive from the southeast. His leadership became central to the early organization and direction of the UN war effort.

By July 3, 41 out of the 59 UN member states had declared support for the Security Council's actions. By mid-September, 29 countries had provided military, economic, or medical support to South Korea. A total of 16 countries—including the United States, United Kingdom, Australia, France, Canada, Turkey, the Philippines, Thailand, Ethiopia, Greece, Colombia, and others—sent combat troops to Korea. Additionally, 6 countries, such as Sweden, Denmark, India, Norway, Italy, and West Germany, provided medical units, and another 38 nations contributed material and humanitarian aid through the UN. In total, 60 countries supported the Republic of Korea during the war or in its aftermath, representing approximately 64% of the world's independent states at the time.

Troop-Contributing Countries

Medical Support Countries

Through these coordinated efforts, the UN's involvement gave the Korean War an unprecedented international character and laid the foundation for future collective security actions under its charter.

Part 2
The Legacy of the Korean War Veterans

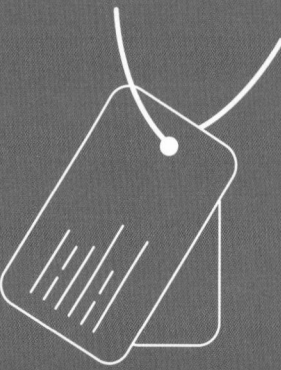

UNITED STATES	Aidan Fleer
	Alexander Pratt
UNITED KINGDOM	Carly Bidwell
AUSTRALIA	Oliver Healy
NETHERLANDS	Leo Schreuders
CANADA	Rachel Cote
NEW ZEALAND	Keishon R. Lynch
THAILAND	Wasita Sritragool
GREECE	Socrates Boutsikaris
SOUTH AFRICA	Alessia Stefanutti
BELGIUM	Lilianne Sourbron
PHILIPPINES	Mary Ellen Burro
	Joon Shin Encomienda Amangan
TÜRKIYE	Ilayda Asımgil
	Eren Yıldırım
LUXEMBOURG	Max Stoffel
COLOMBIA	Stephanie Arguello Gaona
	Valentina Rojas Martinez
Ethiopia	Wakjira Gemechu
	Bethelehem Solomon Shenkute
FRANCE	Alice Prigl d'Ondel
USA / Republic of Korea	Monika Choi Stoy

UNITED STATES

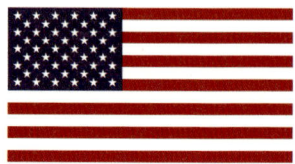

Period of participation	1950.06.27 ~ 1955.03
Total number of troop deployments	1,789,000
Ground Troops	Infantry divisions — 8 Marine division — 1 Regiment combat teams — 2 Troops deployed — 302,483 men
Navy	Naval Forces Far East The 7th Fleet, Task Force 90, Task Force 95
Airforce	Fifth Air Force, Far East Air Forces Bomber Command
Injuries of UN forces attended	KIA — 36,940 WIA — 92,134 MIA — 3,737 POW — 4,439 Total — 137,250

The monument of participation in the Korean War is located in Samok-ri, Munsan-eup, Paju-si, Gyeonggi-do

Those Who Answered the Call to Defend People They Never Met

In memory of Kenneth Fleer

Written by Aidan Fleer

Kenneth Fleer
Air Force Staff Sergeant

Aidan Fleer
Hankuk University of Foreign Studies

About Me

Aidan wearing hanbok, traditional Korean clothing

My name is Aidan Fleer. My journey to living in Korea was shaped by a series of unexpected, interconnected events that I never imagined would become such a defining part of my life. It all started in my first semester of my undergraduate studies at the University of Wisconsin Madison on the first move-in day when I met my roommate Hye-min Kim in the dormitory.

Coming from a small town in Wisconsin, I had never directly interacted with someone this closely who had grown up and embodied the cultural presence of a foreign country such as the Republic of Korea. At first, I was uncertain how this pairing would turn out, but as time went on, we became good friends and were able to share a lot of different perspectives and stories about each other's countries and livelihoods while reveling in typical fashion of young college life.

I majored in Chinese Language and Entrepreneurship Studies so I was already on a path to be engaged in the Eastern Asian countries in a rather intentional and focused mindset compared to that of a regular American's understanding of the region. I had gone on to study abroad in Tianjin, China during my undergraduate studies and also worked in Hong Kong for a short period afterward, then COVID-19 ultimately brought me back to the USA.

In the sporadic and inconsistent communications Hye-min and I had kept over the years past college days, he had remembered my conversation about my grandfather, Kenneth Fleer, who had served in the Korean War. I am sure this conversation was just in passing, but to a Korean, I have come to understand this war and continuing legacy is no light matter. He informed me about the UN Korean War Veteran's Descendants Scholarship while I was in between projects and jobs, hoping to go on a new adventure back to East Asia. I pursued the opportunity, which led to me to get accepted to the scholarship, move to Korea in March 2023, and pursue my studies in Korean language and a Master's degree to begin a new chapter in life.

I currently am starting the third semester of my degree at Hankuk University of Foreign Studies, majoring in International Area Studies with a concentration in International Trade & Commerce. For me, it has been a great opportunity to broaden my horizons and learn about language, culture, and economic zone intimately from the actual ground and birthplace of the people.

USA's Dedication

In the midst of a fragile world shook by the culmination of the end of World War II, the Korean War broke out in a contest between opposing ideologies over the newly liberated region from the Japanese imperialism. During that era, major world powers aligned themselves with opposing sides in the conflict—North Korea received initial support from the Soviet Union and later primarily from China, while South Korea was backed by United Nations member states, mainly from the Western bloc.

Soldier statues at the Korean War Veterans Memorial site in Washington, D.C., USA
"Korean War Veterans Memorial, Washington, D.C." by Carol M. Highsmith, © 2011

However, as the West sought to preserve the newly established Korea under liberal democratic principles rather than communist and socialist ones, the United States emerged as the dominant power—militarily, geographically, and economically—especially since North America remained largely intact and functional, unlike war-ravaged Europe. In this light, through the UN Security Council, the U.S. was named and delegated to command the UN assembled military activities on the Korean Peninsula, headed by Marshal MacArthur, a decorated U.S. military commander from the previous great wars.

The United States' dedication to the war efforts was predominant with approximately 1.8 million men and women in service between 1950 and 1955 and 36,940 casualties during the war. This war became known as "The Forgotten War" because the magnitude of World War II and the subsequent impact of the Vietnam War overshadowed the Korean conflict. The United States' public sentiment at the time wasn't as extreme in favor or in opposition as in the forthcoming Vietnam War, and some have even related it more to a "police action" type of operation.

My Grandfather's Story

Kenneth Fleer at Camp George, Georgia training camp circa in 1951 (first row, 5th from the left)

Kenneth Fleer, born on November 8, 1929, was a very much traditional American man. Having been born in the Midwestern Great Plains state of Missouri, he lived the majority of his days in this state working in the blue-collar trade profession of pipe-fitting and growing a large family of seven children with his beloved wife, Laverne, in a country-side styled fashion. Practical, straightforward, and hardworking with a stern demeanor would be how I would describe him in my own memory. We didn't have a particularly close relationship being the one of many grandchildren, but he always said "stay in school and work hard."

He eventually passed away on May 27, 2020, in his home peacefully, leaving with him many of his Korean War time stories. From my own father's account, the fifth child of my grandfather, he often didn't talk much about his time spent in the service; nevertheless, I have access to several accounts and pieces of information that I can share on his behalf.

For the scholarship, I had to contact the archives of the National Personnel Records Center in St. Louis, Missouri for verification of his service in the Korean War. Unfortunately, there was a large fire in 1973 that destroyed a large portion of records, but I was left with some verifiable information from a "Report of Separation" form from the Armed Forces of the United States.

My grandfather was enlisted in the Air Force in the Air Control & Warning branches, reaching the rank of Staff Sergeant upon his honorable discharge from the Air Force on January 9, 1955. He had a total of 4 years of service among which 2 years 5 months and 7 days were abroad presumably serving in the FEAF [Far East Air Forces]. He was originally trained in radio and telecommunications operations, and therefore served in a support role rather than as a combatant during the war.

After completing his training at Camp Gordon, Georgia, over the span of several months and based on what I could gather from my family members, he was primarily stationed in Fukuoka, Japan—presumably at one of the air control and radio communications stations within the 6160th Air Base Wing. The largest and main air base of the region was the Itazuke Air Base, what is now the current grounds of the Fukuoka airport.

My grandfather's role was in dealing with communications of coordinating plans and relay of information between units, mainly for the air force and navy. He worked with high-speed radio operators and teletype communications, and later became involved in SOJT [Structural on the Job Training] in air traffic control units. What I found particularly interesting was that, as an intelligence officer, his work involved handling highly classified information—often related to planned operations, whether successful or not, and intelligence on enemy activities—making the nature of his role and acquired information highly secretive. I am sure much of that information has been declassified over the decades. Nonetheless, my grandfather, being the stern man he was, didn't like to talk about the affairs he was involved in, so the true nature of those matters remains unknown. He was more open to talk about the times he was off duty, when he was allowed to leave the base in Japan to explore the local area or spend time with fellow soldiers.

He was awarded the Korean Service Medal with two bronze service stars for the following campaigns in Korea: (1) Summer-Fall 1952 Campaign (May 1 to November 30, 1952) and (2) Third Korean Winter Campaign (December 1, 1952 to April 30, 1953), along with several other service medals.

As a side note, my elder brother once wrote an account of our grandfather's service during the Korean War for a scholastic contest, likely around the early to mid-2000s—nearly 20 years ago—and he was chosen as a winner. One vivid memory I have is my brother riding down a large avenue street in the city of Milwaukee, Wisconsin, for a Memorial Day parade in a large military tank adorned in memorabilia with my grandfather in attendance. Seeing that tank, the size comparison with my brother of maybe 12 at that time was an amazing sight to behold as a young boy. The gravity of war and these war machines was something I wouldn't fully grasp until many years later. Though not a glorious war story, this recollection drawn from my brother's memory and his contest submission, remains a meaningful glimpse into that time, and one I felt was worth sharing.

Staff Sergeant Fleer's medals and memorabilia showcase with quote "Our nation honors her sons and daughters who answered the call to defend a country they never knew and a people they never met"

One evening, my grandfather was restless and had

decided to go wash up and brush his teeth in the middle of the night at the latrine area of the barracks. Apparently, this section of the grounds was near the perimeter, and being in his restless state, he stayed out there for some time to catch some fresh air away from the crowded barracks with all the other snoring service-members, perhaps smoking a cigarette or two. Suddenly, he noticed a disturbance in the not-so-far vicinity of where he was standing, a ruffling in the bushes. He slowly and cautiously approached the noise and thought, 'Intruder? Could this possibly be an attack or enemy surveillance on us?' in his head. He prayed that he wouldn't be running back on high-alert to announce enemy activity on the encampment. He got closer and closer, and upon reaching the area, the ruffling stopped, and to his surprise it was nothing other than some animals, perhaps raccoons, bustling about in the night. Through this story, I think

Soldier walking around the barracks

Men in the Air Control & Warning unit working their posts

Undisclosed location, supposedly Korea, near a station Ken was stationed

Aircraft at the Itazuke Airbase, Fukuoka, Japan

My Grandfather's visit to South Korea in 2015

it can be seen as the pervasive paranoia and heightened stress that even people not on the frontlines perceive and feel in the midst of war.

Lastly, my grandfather had the opportunity through one of the veteran's affairs organizations to visit Korea sometime in the mid-2010s to join an inclusive and commemorative Korean War Veterans tour of Korea for a week to enjoy the culture, peace, and prosperity that has been established within the Republic of Korea alongside his wife Laverne. One of my favorite pictures of him is my grandparents dressed in the traditional Korean dress, hanbok, and just knowing how much hospitality and joy they must have received from this commemorative experience. Apparently, they also were shown some of the North Korean underground tunnel networks and even had a picture in the newspaper published from this outing.

A Message to Future Generations

As the number of Korean War veterans dwindles over the eventual tide of time passing, their efforts and service shall not be forgotten. Through memorials, written accounts, memorabilia, and the descendants, their stories live on and have great value for building a future that remembers the pains of war so as not to repeat itself at all costs. I suppose that as a person with such connectivity to this particular war, however so distant, my remembrance, voice, and accounting are important. If anyone else should find themselves in a similar role, it is very much worth the effort to research and share the history that has led to the current paradigm of the world we all live in and share together.

Two War Hero

In memory of Sherman W. Pratt

Written by Alexander Pratt

Sherman W. Pratt
Lieutenant Colonel

Alexander Pratt
Chef

About Me

I am Alexander Pratt, the grandson of Sherman W. Pratt. My grandfather served in the 23rd Infantry Regiment of the 2nd Infantry Division in the Korean War. He served a career in the U.S. Army and retired as a Lieutenant Colonel, having started his Army service as a Private in 1938. I grew up in Florida and I frequently visited my grandparents in Arlington, Virginia. I am currently a chef at a restaurant in Florida, but I studied business administration and worked as an accountant for several years before discovering my true passion. I am also a competitive weightlifter.

As a boy I heard my grandfather's stories from his time in the Army, especially his service in World War II and in the Korean War. My grandfather also published a book on his Korea War experiences titled 'Decisive Battles of the Korean War.'

A book my grandfather wrote in 1992

Although I haven't served in the Army, I greatly appreciate my grandfather's service, and I know he had a remarkable career. He was an avid and accomplished historian and deeply was involved in the project to build the Korean War Veterans Memorial in Washington, D.C. Because of his service in the Korean War, I visited South Korea twice, once sponsored by the Hongbeopsa

With my grandfather, Sherman Pratt (September 2010)

With my father, Paul Pratt, on our revisit to Korea (June 2013)

Buddhist Temple in Busan in 2012 and another visit sponsored by the ROK Ministry of Patriots and Veterans Affairs in 2013. I enjoyed both trips and learned a lot about Korea and Korean culture. I love Korean food for its tasty and complex combination of flavors, textures, and colors.

Because of my grandfather's service in the Korean War in addition to my two visits to Korea including the ROK military units, I have a greater understanding of the Korean War and the importance of the American contribution in the war than most normal Americans my age. I also understand the importance of the alliance between the U.S. and South Korea today, especially with the constant and unpredictable threat posed by North Korea and its large army and nuclear capabilities.

My Grandfather's Story

LTC Sherman Pratt (1959)

My grandfather was born in Tucson, Arizona, and later became an orphan. He joined the Army in 1939 and was stationed in Washington state with the 7th Infantry Regiment of the 3rd Infantry Division. He served the entire Second World War with the regiment and fought in all ten of its campaigns. He served in every enlisted rank from Private to First Sergeant before receiving a battlefield commission in early 1945. As a First Lieutenant, he commanded L Company, 7th Infantry which was one of the two companies to enter Berchtesgaden, Germany, and reach Hitler's Obersalzberg compound and the famous Eagle's Nest. He was promoted to Captain shortly after the war ended and stayed in the Army.

When the Korean War broke out, he reported to the 2nd Infantry Division from his station in Little Rock, Arkansas, where he took command of B Company, 23rd Infantry Regimental Combat Team. He commanded the company in the Battle of the Ch'ongch'on near Kunu-ri, a critical battle on November 29-30, 1950, against the

CPT Sherman Pratt on 38th Parallel (January 1951)

Major Sherman Pratt in the summer of 1951

Chinese. It was a very desperate battle and his combat experience in World War II enabled him to remain calm and in control even at the most critical moments. Not only his superior commanders trusted in his judgment, but his subordinates were inspired to hold on despite overwhelming Chinese numbers.

He was awarded the Silver Star for this action. I have his Silver Star certificate and this is the citation:

The President of the United States of America, authorized by Act of Congress July 9, 1918, takes pleasure in presenting a Bronze Oak Leaf Cluster in lieu of a Second Award of the Silver Star to Captain (Infantry) Sherman Walter Pratt, United States Army, for gallantry in action as a member of Company B, 23d Infantry Regiment, 2d Infantry Division, in action against an armed enemy on 29 and 30 November 1950 in the vicinity of Kunu-ri, Korea. On the night of 29 and 30 November 1950, he was assigned the mission of holding commanding terrain to cover the withdrawal of elements of the division. In the early morning hours on November 30, 1950 his defensive position was attacked by a numerically superior enemy force, which inflicted many casualties among his men. By skillfully shifting his men from one point to another as the attacks occurred, Captain Pratt was able to meet and repel each assault upon his positions. With complete disregard for his own safety, he constantly exposed himself to the intense enemy fire and personally directed all phases of the defense. By his forceful and inspiring leadership, he was able to hold his remaining men together and successfully defend the position. The gallantry and competent leadership displayed by Captain Pratt on this occasion reflect great credit upon himself and the military service.

My grandfather's performance led to his moving up to being the Battalion Operations Officer for his battalion, the 1st Battalion of the 23rd Regimental Combat Team. In this position he planned the battalion's activities and coordinated for all necessary support. It is the third most important position in the unit behind the battalion commander and the battalion executive officer.

While serving in this position, he participated in the Battle of Heartbreak Ridge; this battle was a critical victory against the NKPA [North Korean People's Army], from September 13 to October 15, 1951. The area was in the vicinity of Chorwon. The NKPA was occupying extensive defensive positions after having been defeated in an earlier battle named Bloody Ridge. My grandfather was responsible for the successful attack plan which his battalion followed. Shortly after this battle, my grandfather was promoted to Major and moved up to serve as the Regimental Executive Officer for the 23rd Infantry Regiment. After a year in combat, my grandfather left Korea and continued his Army career.

My Grandfather after the Korean War

After returning to the United States from his service in the Korean War, my grandfather continued to serve in the Army.

While still in the Army, my grandfather earned his law degree through night school at the University of Arkansas at Little Rock. After he retired from the Army in 1959, he worked as a contract lawyer for the Federal Communications Commission. He was active in the 2nd Infantry Division Association and traveled to Korea several times to participate in historical terrain walks with officers from the 2nd Infantry Division which was stationed in Korea. He was an avid yachtsman and a great adventurer. He drove his sports car the entire length of Africa.

He was deeply involved in the fundraising and building of the Korean War Veterans Memorial on the Mall in Washington, DC. As a member of the Korean War Veterans Association, he was a frequent contributor to the association's newsletter, "The Graybeard." He was also an avid local historian, publishing a history of Arlington, Virginia. My grandfather died September 23, 2013, at the age of 91. He is buried in Arlington National Cemetery.

Sherman Pratt sailing sometime in the 1960s

Message to the Younger Generation

Everyone should visit the Republic of Korea to appreciate the great achievements of the South Korean people over the past 72 years. The Republic of Korea stands as both a testament to a modern-day miracle and the result of the unwavering dedication and hard work of successive generations of South Koreans. At the same time, everyone must remember the sacrifices made by the men and women who fought, bled, and died to keep South Korea free, enabling this miracle. These sacrifices reflect the deep bond and enduring love the United States has shown toward Korea—an expression of solidarity that must never be forgotten. We owe our deepest gratitude to the veterans who made this possible.

Visiting my grandfather's grave in Arlington National Cemetery in November 2024

UNITED KINGDOM

Period of participation	1950.06.29 ~ 1957
Total number of troop deployments	81,084
Ground Troops	Infantry brigades 2 Marine commando 1 Troops deployed 14,198 men
Navy	Total: 52 vessels (including 5 aircraft carriers)
Injuries of UN forces attended	KIA 1,106 WIA 2,674 MIA 179 POW 978 Total 4,937

The monument of participation in the Korean War is located in Seolma-ri, Jeoksong-myeon, Paju-si, Gyeonggi-do

Our Hero

In memory of Derek Anthony Bidwell

Written by Carly Bidwell

Derek Anthony Bidwell
Leading signalman

Carly Bidwell
Deputy Headteacher, Hampshire

About Me

Derek Anthony Bidwell
RN No. 890293
Born: 16th August 1935

Growing up, both my siblings and I felt so proud that Derek was our grandfather because he didn't seem to be much like anyone else's grandfather! We knew that he had been in the Navy as his house was filled with memorabilia, but also, he and my other family members would always 'toast the Queen' with some Navy rum when we went to visit after 'welcoming us aboard!'

Later in life, my grandad, affectionately known as the 'Admiral' by his friends, took up flying. He taught cadets and excitable family members, myself included to fly! All of my family have been taken flying by him and I particularly enjoyed it when he used to do aerobatics. He flew Cessna planes with cadets as well as a Yak and a Tiger Moth plane. I was always so proud to have such a cool grandfather and I think his military and flying background has rubbed off on much of my family. I became an Air Cadet and went through officer selection at RAF Cranwell. Not only did he fly, he was also there when my brother and I were swimming and diving in Southend-on-Sea galas. As you will read later, he was quite a swimmer and diver himself!

I am now a Deputy Headteacher in a secondary school and teach History. Although neither of this are strictly related to the work my grandfather did, I do have pictures of him in my office and our annual Remembrance event at school always has him at the centre, leading the school Roll of Honour.

Derek Bidwell and his seven grandchildren, from left to right: Amie Cheveralls, Luke Cheveralls, Carly Bidwell, Cooper Bidwell, Ben Cheveralls, Adam Bidwell, Harry Bidwell. Portsmouth, England. (2017)

United Kingdom and the Korean War

The United Kingdom was involved in the Korean War from June 29, 1950, up until 1953. 81,084 British troops participated on the side of the United Nations force. The United Kingdom provided the second largest force behind the United States. For deployment, the Royal Navy arrived on July 1, 1950, whilst the British Army arrived on August 28. During the war, 1106 of our soldiers were killed. 886 of them were buried in the United Nations Memorial Cemetery, Busan, South Korea. After the war, some British troops remained as military observers until 1957. On December 3, 2014, a Korean War Memorial was unveiled in London.

Ethel, Helen, Derek and Charles Bidwell

Derek Bidwell, HMS Ganges (1950)

Derek Bidwell and other Korean Veterans (2018)

My Grandfather's Story

Grandad was born on August 16, 1935. He was born in Welling and enjoyed model making, once building a wooden sailboat that even had detailed rigging and sails sewn by his mother. He used to visit Damson Park swimming pool and lake where he sailed the boat and sunk it with an air rifle. Before joining the Navy, he took art and music lessons and learned the violin.

Derek, or grandad to his seven grandchildren and now great-grandfather to two, was only 14 years old when he signed up to the Royal Navy on November 14, 1950. His father didn't want him in the Navy, but his mother persuaded him to sign the papers for HMS Ganges [Her Majesty's Ship, a prefix used for ships in the British Royal Navy]. He started his training at HMS Ganges in North Essex where he became a water polo player, diver (high board), and swimmer. On his first day, he had to undergo medical checks and everyone had their hair cut in a standard cut. Before they were issued with their uniform, they had to have a shower. The shower block was the opposite side of the parade ground to his dormitory. The boys had nothing to wear but a towel and had to run across the parade ground in the freezing cold November wind and rain to get to the shower block! He was offered the opportunity to convert to officer training but

Derek Bidwell onboard in the Far East

Far Derek Bidwell (far right) onboard HMS Newcastle with the Communications Team

wanted to stay with his ship mates. He had his 17th birthday in Malta, onboard HMS Birmingham, enroute to the Korean War. He wasn't old enough to drink, so instead he celebrated with a 7UP! At sea, the Chief Petty Officer asked if there were any artists on board, grandad naturally volunteered his services and was immediately assigned painting the ship.

His first experience onboard a ship was going to war in Korea. Once in Korean waters, there was a time when everyone was locked into their compartments as there were anti shipping mines in the water. This is done for damage control, so if the hull is compromised by an explosion, it only floods a few compartments. My grandad was then locked up in his bunk waiting until all the mines had been cleared. It must have been terrifying.

He was a signalman and a very good one; he was tasked with bringing the leading

Derek at an event held in honor of Korean War veterans in Kingston-upon-Thames

Carly, Derek, and Adam Bidwell on Remembrance Day, London. (2010)

signalman on the Admiralty's fleet at one time. As a signalman, he was also the Radio Operator in shore parties. In the 1950's, the portable radio sets were very large so he wasn't able to carry a rifle. Instead, he was given a 45 pistol. They had to travel up a river in an open boat to pick up a South Korean agent. Suddenly, a man jumped out of the bushes, and everyone thought they were about to be machine-gunned, but it turned out to be the friendly agent. Phew!

Once, grandad and his shipmates saw an allied aircraft do an emergency landing, and before it went in, it jettisoned its' load of rockets. The rockets stuck in the sand along a beach and grandad was in group tasked with going ashore to dispose of them. No one was really an expert in rocket demolition and the first charge blew them off their feet. After that, they used less explosives and retired behind the sand dunes.

He also told me that when he was on board, he heard his ship firing at Korea, he said that the ship would ring a bell, then boom, the guns then exploded. He said that they were so loud and that the ship shook. If they fired a broadside the ship would shift back in the water.

My grandad never really dwelled on the fact that things were scary. He told my brothers and I when he also used to jive onboard to Elvis. In fact, I seem to remember him saying he was listening to 'Jail House Rock' when he heard the news that my father, Paul was born.

Grandad served on both HMS Newcastle and HMS Birmingham when he was in Korea. Newcastle was tasked with patrols, carrier escorts, and providing naval gunfire support to UN forces. In June 1952, as the Panmunjom (Korea) negotiations moved belatedly towards an armistice, HMS Birmingham, along with the cruiser Newcastle and two frigates, supported American landing craft evacuating thousands of friendly Koreans from islands off the north-west coast. An armistice was finally reached in June 1953. In June 1954, Birmingham returned home from the Far East.

My grandad was an excellent swimmer and diver. He used to swim with my brother and I, teaching us how to dive, swim underwater, and watch me compete in swimming galas. With my family's love of swimming, he once told my brothers and I of when he swam in the Far East. He said that the ship's company was allowed some R&R (Rest and Recuperation) and all went overboard to swim. Sometime after that, he then looked down and noticed sharks swimming underneath him! I also spoke to my uncle, Jason, who recalled another shark story. Once, my grandad and his mates got a large tin from the galley, filled it with kitchen waste, and threw it over the side on a thick cable. They hauled a large shark on deck and everyone went to have a look. As they got there, the shark opened its jaws like it was doing a massive yawn, so the PTI (Physical Training Instructor) clubbed it to death with an exercise club!

During his time in the Navy, grandad served on HMS Cheviot, HMS Bramble, HMS Northumberland, HMS Bulwark and HMS Birmingham.

After Korea, Grandad did two tours of the Far East, based at Sasebo Japan. He returned to the UK to be assigned to HMS Bramble, a minesweeper operating in Artic waters. He then joined the Admiralty Staff to be nearer his family and was assigned Naval Quarters in Tulse Hill, where his second child, Karen, was born. He enlisted for a full 16-year commitment: 4 years as a boy seaman, followed by 12 years as a regular seaman, and left by 1964. He left as a leading signalmen and marksman.

The Korean Government was always very grateful for the UN's help in the war. Grandad was issued a retrospective Korean War Service medal by the South Korean Government. A South Korean Admiral visited the RNA [Royal Navy Association] in Southend every year and grandad got to know him on first name terms. We often wondered how long that Korean Admiral spent visiting small Naval Associations around the UK and if they had Admirals doing that in all the countries who helped them in the war. I once was lucky enough to meet an Admiral, too when I marched in the National Remembrance Day Parade with my grandfather on a few occasions. He was immaculately dressed and so polite.

I am so proud that Derek Bidwell was my grandfather, I think of him and miss him always.

Derek Bidwell teaching cadets to fly circa (1990)

Derek, Carly, and Harry Bidwell on Remembrance Day, London (2015)

Derek Bidwell flying

A message to Future Generations

2025 marks 75 years since the start of the Korean War, a war that has never formally ended, and many believe has been forgotten. Yet for those who fought, endured its hardships, and live with its legacy, the Korean War remains unforgettable.

To me, my grandfather was a hero, and his memory will live on through my family. To all the other families whose grandfathers travelled to the other side of the world to fight for peace and freedom, they were also heroes. Some of these men gave their lives for a country, that until they arrived there, they had never even heard of.

Do not let their sacrifices be in vain. Honour their memories, reflect with pride the role that they all played in securing freedom for South Korea, on which a vibrant, dynamic, and democratic society has been built. Celebrate the successes of our countries' long and enduring friendship and our commitment to upholding peace.

AUSTRALIA

Period of participation	1950.06.29 ~ 1957.08
Total number of troop deployments	17,164
Ground Troops	Infantry battalions 2 Troops deployed 2,282 men
Navy	Total: 4 vessels
Airforce	1 Fighter Squadron 1 Transport Aircraft Squadron
Injuries of UN forces attended	KIA 340 WIA 1,216 POW 30 Total 1,586

The monument of participation in the Korean War is located in Yungnae-ri, Gapyeong-gun, Gapyeong-eup, Gyeonggi-do

Across the Water:
Remembering My Great Uncle

In memory of Vince Healy

Written by Oliver Healy

Vince Healy
Sergeant

Oliver Healy
Queensland University of Technology

About Me

G'day! My name is Oliver Healy and I'm a 20-year-old from the beautiful state of Queensland, Australia. Growing up, surrounded by the stunning landscapes of the Sunshine Coast and the tropical vibe of the Great Barrier Reef, I've always had a deep connection to nature and the outdoors. I feel incredibly lucky to live in such a vibrant place, where beach days, hiking trails, and camping under the stars are just part of everyday life. Queensland has shaped who I am today and I'm proud to call this place my home.

When I'm not out and about exploring, you can find me hanging out with my mates, listening to music, or enjoying a good meal at one of Queensland's many amazing food spots. I'm currently in my second year of studying Architecture at the Queensland University of Technology and I have hopes of studying overseas for my final year.

I'm always up for discovering new places. So, in early 2023, when the Korean embassy here in Australia reached out to my family asking if I wanted to spend a week in a different country, I jumped at the opportunity. Getting a chance to reflect and appreciate my great uncle Vince, who fought and passed away in the Korean War, was an

Oliver Healy, Chris Healy, Piper Healy, QLD Australia, family photo (2015)

Oliver Healy and Isabella Setefano, NSW Australia, family reunion (2025)

Oliver Healy, QLD Australia, camping near the beach (2025)

experience I will cherish forever. That trip abroad sparked new friendships with people I would have never met otherwise, and I can't thank those who looked after me enough.

I'm someone who values positivity, growth, and learning. As a young adult, I'm still figuring things out, but I've learned to embrace the journey and enjoy the ride. I've always believed that life is about the connections we make and the impact we leave on others. Whether it's through making new friends, a shared laugh, or working on a project together, I believe that we all have something to offer, and the most meaningful things are often the simplest.

Looking ahead, I'm excited about what the future holds. I'm open to new opportunities, both professionally and personally, and I'm eager to meet like-minded individuals who share my passions and dreams. My goal is to keep growing, learning, and making the most of every moment.

Australia's Dedication

Australia's involvement in the Korean War marked a significant chapter in our history, one that reflects our commitment to global peace, security, and strong

Oliver Healy, Ilayda Asimgil, Keishon lynch, Simon Kornfeld, UN descendants camp, Seoul, South Korea (2023)

Oliver Healy, UN descendants camp, United Nations Memorial Cemetery, Busan, South Korea (2023)

international partnerships. As a proud member of the Commonwealth, Australia answered the call to support South Korea in 1950, when North Korea's invasion threatened the stability of the Korean Peninsula. A conflict that would go on to last three years, it saw the loss of many lives but also highlighted Australia's enduring dedication to its allies and principles of freedom and democracy.

When the war broke out, Australia swiftly sent troops, ships, and airmen to assist the United Nations forces. More than 17,000 Australians including my Great uncle served in Korea between 1950 and 1953, with Vince along with 340 men and woman losing their lives in the conflict. The courage and sacrifice of our soldiers were nothing short of extraordinary. Australian troops, alongside those from other nations, helped to push back the North Korean forces and protect South Korea from communist expansion. The role of the Australian forces in the battlefields of places like Kapyong and the significant support given by the Royal Australian Navy and the Royal Australian Air Force were crucial to the success of the UN mission.

Australia's contributions went beyond just military support. Throughout the war, we were committed to offering humanitarian assistance to the people of South Korea, helping them rebuild after the devastation of war. This dedication reflected the compassion and

Vincent Healy, Kathleen Healy, QLD Australia (1930)

Vincent Healy and Thelma Healy (Vinces's mother), QLD Australia, before he volunteered to fight in the Korean War

Vincent Healy, QLD Australia, state pole vault champion (1948)

sense of duty that Australia has long upheld on the global stage. The bond formed during the Korean War laid the foundation for a lasting and meaningful relationship between Australia and South Korea, one built on mutual respect and shared values.

Fast forward to today, the relationship between the two countries remains as strong as ever. In the decades since the Korean War, Australia and South Korea have grown into close allies and partners in various fields. Our ties are evident in trade, culture, security, and education. South Korea is one of Australia's key trading partners, with our two countries cooperating across a broad spectrum of sectors, including technology, energy, agriculture, and defence. The people-to-people connections have only deepened, with thousands of South Korean students studying in Australia and many Australians traveling to South Korea, strengthening the cultural ties between us.

Our shared values, including democracy, the rule of law, and a commitment to peace, continue to guide our collaboration today. The diplomatic relationship between Australia and South Korea remains strong, with ongoing cooperation on regional and global security issues, including efforts to maintain peace in the Indo-Pacific region. Australia has been a strong supporter of South Korea's security, working together through alliances like the United Nations Command and through regional multilateral

Thelma Healy, Busan, South Korea, visiting Vince's grave (1961)

Sgt Vincent Healy, 3RAR, killed in action (1951)

Vincent J Healy, Busan, South Korea, United Nations Memorial Cemetery (2023)

forums such as the East Asia Summit.

In every way, the bond that was formed in the heat of the Korean War has persisted. Australia's commitment to South Korea back in the 1950s was more than just military; it was about standing up for what is right, and that same spirit of support and friendship continues today. As both nations move forward into an ever-changing world, the alliance between Australia and South Korea stands as a testament to the enduring power of cooperation, respect, and shared values. Our connection, forged in the fires of war, is now a shining example of how two nations, despite being oceans apart, can build something lasting and meaningful together.

My Grandfather, Vince Healy

Born on the August 5, 1926, in Brisbane, Australia, Vincent Joseph Healy was the 1st of 9 kids of the Healy family. Being the eldest, Vince took on the huge responsibility of helping to raise and look after his mom and eight siblings. Vince later went through school achieving a higher education while also playing and competing in multiple athletic sports. At age 22, Vince won the poll vault state title with a jump of 3.27 metres during the Queensland Amateur athletic association carnival. He also came second in the 220-yard hurdles for the same competition. Vince was a self-taught pole vaulter who practiced from his home and to go on and win a state title was an amazing feat.

On December 1, 1944, Vince enlisted the Australian armed forces and served in the post war efforts of World War II. later on, Vince became a sergeant and joined the Korean War with the medium machine gun platoon 3RAR [3rd Battalion Royal Australian Regiment], arriving to Busan on September 28, 1950. Just one year later, 24-year-old Vincent Healy was killed in action trying to assist his fellow comrade who was injured. Vince went forward, away from cover, to carry the injured soldier to safety where he was then struck by a piece of mortar in the head killing him instantly. The injured soldier went on to survive the incident.

Vince died the way he lived, helping and looking after those he loved. He was buried in Busan in South Korea and was 1 of the 340 Australians to lose their life during the conflict. His family back in Australia grieved his passing, his mother Thelma Healy decided to make the pilgrimage overseas to see her son's final resting place after the war had died down. Decades later, members of the Healy family including myself have followed in her footsteps in coming to South Korea to visit Vince's grave and pay our respects. In the years to come, I hope that our children's children will be able to do the same and see the country our ancestor died protecting.

Thelma's journey to Busan is documented detailing the story in Louise Evans' book, 'Passage to Pusan'.

Message to Future Generations

To the future generations, I hope that you can gain something from my family member's story; Vince lived his life to the fullest and took care of those around him, not because he had to, but because it was the right thing to do. Going out into this big ever-changing world is scary at times, but I've found that tackling things with a positive mindset makes traversing life not as terrifying. Unfortunately, it's easier to be selfish than to do the right thing nowadays, but in spite of that, I hope you all will choose to help each other out when things get hard.

To Vince, you've been an inspiration to our whole family and I thank you for your service in helping those around you. In 2025, you'd be 99 years old and I wish I could have met you. Your sacrifice along with all fallen soldiers helps provide a better tomorrow for South Korea and all nations of the United Nations. Thank you.

NETHERLANDS

Period of participation	1950.07.16 ~ 1955.01	
Total number of troop deployments	5,322	
Ground Troops	Infantry battalions Troops deployed	1 819 men
Navy	Destroyer: 1	
Injuries of UN forces attended	KIA WIA Total	120 645 768

The monument of participation in the Korean War is located in Uhang-ri, Uchon-myeon, Hoengseong-gun, Gangwon-do

The Story of My Father, Korean War Veteran Colonel Leendert Schreuders

In memory of Leendert Schreuders

Written by Leo Schreuders

Leendert Schreuders
Colonel

Leo Schreuders
secretary-general of the KWVA VOKS

About Me

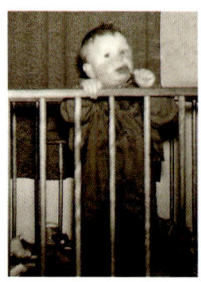

A photo of me from my childhood (July 1954)

Being the fourth child of my parents, I was born on July 25, 1953, in Weert, located in the south of the Netherlands. My mother was English and after their marriage, she and my father went to live in the town Utrecht in the Netherlands.

Our family grew to six children and the atmosphere at home was always very enjoyable. Although my father was quite strict, he had everything to spare for his wife and children. Because of his work as a military officer, he was transferred each time after a promotion. That meant we often had to move. In total, I moved with my parents seven times, on average every two to three years, both within the Netherlands, to Germany, and to SHAPE [Supreme Headquarters Allied Powers Europe] in Belgium. At the time, we thought that was quite normal; we did not know any better.

Unlike my father, I eventually decided not to opt for a career in the army. After primary and secondary school, I was still called up for military service, which I completed in the Air Force at Eindhoven Air Base.

Schreuders family picture (2013)

After that, I had great jobs. I became a teacher, a tour guide abroad in Greece, Tunisia, Spain, and the Caribbean, and after that, a driving school owner. Then, I worked as a manager at the driving school's department of the national organization BOVAG [Bond van Garagehouders] and eventually as a driving examiner at the CBR [Centraal Bureau Rijvaardigheidsbewijzen]. I retired in 2019.

In 1981, I married Marianne and together we had two children. Our daughter has worked at the Police Forensic Investigation Department in The Hague for many years and continues to do so today, while our son is now a captain in the Royal Military Police. We are also blessed with two grandchildren: a nine-year-old granddaughter and a six-month-old granddaughter.

My father founded the VOKS [Korean War Veterans Association of The Netherlands] in 1977, and I was thus given a significant role in organizing commemorations and reunions for Korean War veterans.

When my father was no longer able to run the association due to his advanced age, I took over these duties as secretary-general of the KWVA VOKS. I took care of the annual revisits for Korean War veterans, arranged funerals at the United Nations Cemetery in Busan for those who wanted to be buried there, published the magazine VOX-V.O.K.S. for our members, and provided information to relatives about their father or grandfather who had fought in Korea for that country's freedom. I did all this in close cooperation with the Embassy of the Republic of Korea in the Netherlands, the Embassy of The Netherlands in Seoul, and the MPVA [Ministry of Patriots and Veterans Affairs] in Korea.

In recognition of our contribution to the Republic of Korea's freedom and democracy, our KWVA VOKS received in July 2020 the highly respected Presidential Unit Citation from ROK President Moon Jae-in.

In April 2024, I was incredibly surprised and honored to receive a high Royal decoration, namely Knight of the Order of Orange-Nassau, for my commitment and work for the Korean War Veterans.

Netherlands' Dedication

When the Korean War broke out in 1950, the Netherlands decided to voluntarily contribute to the liberation of South Korea. On October 15, 1950, the NDVN [Netherlands Detachment United Nations] was established. All soldiers within this detachment were assigned to the Van Heutsz Regiment.

A total of 4,746 men from the Dutch Army and Navy participated in the liberation action of South Korea. These men had diverse motives: they wanted to fight against communism, were looking for adventure, had no work in the Netherlands, or saw an opportunity for a job as a professional soldier after their return.

The first detachment left on October 26, 1950, with the ship 'SS Zuiderkruis' and consisted of 636 men. My father was part of this first detachment.

The men of the NDVN were deployed to the front almost immediately by arrival in Korea, and often found themselves in combat situations, and were constantly on patrol. They worked under very harsh conditions: winters were bitterly cold, rain was frequent, and the roads were in poor condition.

The soldiers included former paratroopers and commandos of the Special Forces

The Dutch graves at the United Nationals Memorial Cemetery

Regiment, including the commander of the NDVN, Lieutenant-Colonel Den Ouden. He was killed in the attack on Hoengseong on February 12, 1951.

A total of 26 Dutch supplementary detachments took part in this war. The last unit returned to the Netherlands in December 1954. In addition, the Dutch Royal Navy contributed with six naval vessels that were part of the US 7th Fleet and deployed in Korean waters.

Also, three Dutch naval officers were assigned to the 807th Squadron on the British aircraft carrier HMS (Her Majesty's Ship, a prefix used for Royal Navy ships of the United Kingdom) Ocean. They departed from Malta in April 1953 and arrived in Sasebo, Japan, on May 17, 1953. There, they conducted operations with the single-seat fighter Hawker Seafury FB 11 in the Yellow Sea from May 17 to November 1, 1953.

During the Korean War, the NDVN lost 120 men, whom were killed, perished by accident or disease, or died in captivity.

In Busan, on the Dutch part of the UNMCK, United Nations Memorial Cemetery in Korea, there are 123 graves: 117 for the fallen Dutch soldiers and six empty graves.

Illustration of my father

My father and I, in the Netherlands (2015)

First Lieutenant Leendert Schreuders on Hill 325 (February 1951)

These empty graves are for two soldiers who could not be recovered and three whose fate is unknown.

One person fell overboard when the naval vessel Hr.Ms. (Harer Majesteits, Dutch for "Her Majesty's") Piet Hein set sail from Den Helder and drowned, one is buried at the Honor Cemetery in Loenen (Gld.), and another in Singapore at Kanji Field of Honor.

My Father's Story

My father was born on October 25, 1923, in Utrecht. He was the eldest child in a family with a brother and a sister. After completing High School, he was able to work in the factory of his father, located in the small village of Heerewaarden.

At the beginning of World War II, after the German invasion, my father joined the resistance against the German occupiers. His resistance group was betrayed, with almost all members being arrested and shot by the Germans. However, my father managed to escape and was the only one from his group to survive.

After liberation, he had only one wish: to become a soldier. He therefore enlisted in the army and left for the Dutch East Indies in 1947. Shortly before, he had met his future wife Eileen during his officer training in Britain.

During a patrol in the Dutch East Indies (South Sumatra), his unit was attacked by armed Indonesian groups. My father fought back with a pistol, took out some enemies and forced the attackers to flee. For this brave act, he later received the prestigious royal 'Bronze Lion' award.

In March 1950, Lieutenant Schreuders returned to the Netherlands and saw his now 18-month-old son for the first time. Although his wife Eileen hoped he would now stay home, the Korean War broke out in June 1950, leading to Lieutenant Schreuders' decision to rejoin the liberation of South Korea.

Eileen struggled to understand his decision. Her husband barely knew his son, and if he died, who would take care of her and their child? Yet she did not stop him. The army was his passion and, besides, he would have a chance to get a position as a professional soldier after his return.

On October 26, 1950, a day after his 27th birthday, he left on the ship 'SS Zuiderkruis' for Korea, along with the first Dutch Detachment United Nations, which consisted of 636 soldiers. On arrival, they were brought to Suwon by train and were given temporary accommodation at the Samil School in the city of Suwon. From 1980 onwards, the KWVA VOKS developed a special relationship with this school, which has been maintained by our association until today.

During his deployment as a platoon commander in Korea, Lieutenant Schreuders also escaped death. While sleeping in a makeshift foxhole, he was summoned to the commander's office. He got up, walked a few steps outside, after which a grenade hit his foxhole, piercing his sleeping bag.

Another of his memories was a deployment at Hill 325. He was ordered to throw grenades into a cave with his platoon because enemy troops were said to be there. My father did not trust this and decided to look for himself. He discovered they were not enemies but elderly men, women, and children, so he managed to avoid a massacre.

On February 12, 1951, he found himself in the Hoengseong area. The commander, Lieutenant Colonel Den Ouden, sent my father and his platoon to Hill 325 to investigate the situation. It turned out afterwards that Hoengseong was attacked by the Chinese, in which 17 Dutch soldiers lost their lives, including commander Den Ouden. With that, my father escaped this attack.

Nine soldiers died during the Chinese attack on Hill 325. My father escaped death again when a shell exploded close to his position.

In October 1951, my father returned to the Netherlands. He then started his career as a professional officer and finished his service in the rank of colonel.

At home, my father hardly spoke about his experiences during the Korean War. He found little room to share his story with the family, as did many other soldiers of the

NDVN. For this reason, together with General Tack, also a Korean War veteran of the first detachment in Korea, he founded the VOKS [Korean War Veterans Association of The Netherlands].

Within this association, Dutch soldiers who had fought in Korea could share their experiences with each other. For his commitment to Dutch veterans in general and specifically to Korean War veterans, he received the Gold Badge of Honour, our country's highest military decoration, on his retirement from the board of VOKS in 2010. The award was handed over by the deputy commander of the army, Major General De Kruif.

Mrs. Eileen Schreuders died in 2013, and her husband, Colonel Leendert Schreuders, followed her in 2017. According to the wishes of both, they were cremated and their ashes were spread from a boat on the North Sea by their six children. This sea is the connection between England, Eileen's native country, and the Netherlands, where Leendert came from.

A Message to the Future Relationship

People, including both men and women, committed themselves to a country far from their safe lives and performed heroic deeds there. I have been to Korea twice and experienced how the people honour and remember our Korea War veterans.

Foreign Korean War veterans are greeted warmly, often with a handshake or hug, both by older Koreans and their children and grandchildren. Their deeds are passed down from generation to generation in South Korea. In our country, the Korean War was often called 'The Forgotten War'. It was rarely mentioned in Dutch history books, seldom discussed, and largely overlooked. This caused great sorrow to our Dutch Korea War veterans, as they fought for the freedom of South Korea.

With these words, I address the current generation and those that come after us.

Peace is never simply given—it must be earned and protected. Today's world reminds us of this more than ever. If we continue to resist oppression and work for peace, things must eventually work out. We owe our heartfelt gratitude to those who fought for South Korea's freedom. It's up to our generation to remember this once-forgotten war and to ensure its story lives on through the generations to come.

Colonel Schreuders receiving the Gold Badge of Honour (2010)

CANADA

Period of participation	1950.07.25 ~ 1957.06
Total number of troop deployments	26,791
Ground Troops	Infantry brigade 1 Forces 6,164 men
Navy	Destroyer: 3
Air Force	Transport Flying Unit: 1
Injuries of UN forces attended	KIA 516 WIA 1,212 MIA 1 POW 32 Total 1,761

The monument of participation in the Korean War is located in Yigok-ri, Buk-myeon, Gapyeong-gun, Gyeonggi-do

Bridging Generations:
A Canadian Veteran's Story and Korea's Lasting Honor

In memory of Bernard Cote

Written by Rachel Cote

Bernard Cote
Lance corporal

Rachel Cote
University of Windsor

About Me

Rachel Cote, UN Peace Ambassador, Peace Camp (2024)

Growing up, my grandfather was very hesitant to share stories about his experiences in Korea with us. He found it difficult to ever speak about the war, as that time was very difficult for him. Instead, I was able to learn about Korea through exploring his home as a child. He was very proud of Korea as a nation. From the moment he arrived home from the war until the day he passed, he flew the Taegeukgi, the national flag of South Korea, proudly in his backyard. All throughout the walls of his home, he had memorabilia displayed: pictures, medals, maps, barbed wire from the DMZ, and so much more. Because of this, from a very young age I knew that we had a special connection to Korean culture, I just didn't quite understand the full extent of it. When I was 9, the Ministry of Veterans and Patriots Affairs connected me with a pen pal from Korea. We exchanged letters and small gifts every few weeks. To this day, I still have all of the small toys she sent me and think about her every so often. This was such a special way to connect Canadian youth to the people of Korea.

As we got older, he began to open up more and share his memories from the war. I loved learning about Korea through him. My favorite memories with him were sitting

Rachel Cote, Gyeongbokgung Palace (2024)

Rachel Cote, representing UN Peace Ambassador with the Vice Minister of the MPVA Lee Hee-wan (2024)ⓒ 세계일보

in his living room, flipping through all of his photo albums from back then, and going through his belongings. While he avoided talking about the war, his face would light up with happiness whenever we discussed Korea and how far it had come. I quickly fell in love with Korean culture and began to completely immerse myself. From dramas to K-pop, I even began taking language classes in an attempt to appreciate the culture more. Through my grandfather, the opportunity arose for me to attend the annual MPVA Peace Camp in Korea a few summers ago. This experience changed my life. Going to Korea and seeing how much it had changed in just 72 years was both shocking and inspiring, filling me with pride for the Korean people. During the camp, I had the opportunity to visit the places my grandfather had once been and create lifelong friendships with descendants just like me from all over the world. Ever since this experience, it has become my dream to move to Korea, continue my education, and start a career giving back to the veterans.

Canada and The Korean War

When the Korean War erupted in 1950, the Canadian Army's call to action came, leaving them with a choice: stay home and watch from afar or to step up. Over 26,000 Canadians answered the call, braving an unforgiving and unfamiliar landscape thousands of miles away from home, fighting a war that many at the time barely even understood. But for the soldiers of the 2 PPCLI [2nd Battalion Princess Patricia's Canadian Light Infantry], this was more than just another deployment. It was a test of sheer will, courage, and brotherhood, one that would forever etch their names into history.

Nothing proved their bravery more than the Battle of Kapyong, a desperate, all-or-nothing stand against an overwhelming Chinese offensive in April 1951. Outnumbered nearly seven to one, with just 700 Canadians against over 5,000 Chinese troops, the Patricias dug in on Hill 677, knowing that if they fell, the road to Seoul would be wide open to enemy forces. The battle raged for three relentless days and nights with the hungry and sleep-deprived soldiers, holding their ground with nothing but determination. Yet, against impossible odds, the PPCLI held the line. Their unwavering resistance halted the enemy's advance and saved countless lives, earning them the U.S. Presidential Unit Citation, a rare and profound honor for a non-American force. The PPCLI were the only non-American force to ever receive this medal in history. However, the cost was steep; many never returned home. Those who did carried the weight of what they had seen and endured for the rest of their lives.

2 PPCLI D Company, Lance Corporal Bernard Cote is seen in the middle row, third person from the left (1950)

Bernard Cote (right) you can see where he drew an arrow pointing to himself in the photo, setting up artillery on the front lines (1950)

Bernard Cote (center back, smoking a cigarette) on April 25, 1951, the day after the Battle of Kapyong, when a relatively small number of Canadian soldiers held off a vastly superior number of enemy troops from positions atop a rocky ridge dubbed Hill 677

Bernard Cote (right), Busan (1951)

Bernard Cote, right, PPCLI base camp in Busan

My Grandfather's Stories and Memories

Unlike today, back in 1950, South Korea was an unheard-of nation. It quickly became miles and miles of a war-torn country, filled with nothing but horror and sadness. The condition of Korea when my grandfather arrived really seemed to bother him, as this was something he often brought up. He said that he could not believe his eyes when he got there, there was just nothing. Everything had been destroyed, and for miles and miles, all you could see were families displaced with nowhere to go, carrying everything they owned on their backs. He said little babies were walking through rubble, some with parents, others sadly without. For a young Private Bernard Cote, this was an incomprehensible reality.

The night of the Battle of Kapyong, my grandfather's platoon had just returned from holding off troops elsewhere. The call that was supposed to come through relieving them, instead directed them to Hill 677. My grandfather said that he and the other soldiers had not slept or eaten in days and were freezing from being wet in the trenches. The march to Kapyong was quiet and filled with anxiety; the soldiers unknowing of what lay ahead. On the way up the hill, he recalled stepping over bodies that were left for dead and trying to gather as many dog tags as he could. During the battle, for three

Bernard Cote visiting the grave of his fellow comrade who lost his life fighting alongside the PPCLI at the young age of 21, UNMCK (2014)

Bernard Cote with his Grandson Jakob Cote on the Revisit Korea trip (2014)

straight days and nights, all you could hear was shots being fired, bombs dropped, and artillery shells flying everywhere. It was pure and unthinkable chaos. After the battle, the first thing my grandfather remembered was when the troops were finally relieved from Hill 677, they were given blankets and a cup of steaming dakjuk, a Korean porridge with chicken. For the shell-shocked soldiers, this would be the only thing their bodies could handle eating after being starved for days. Ever since that day, my grandfather became so attached to dakjuk that he would continue to eat it almost every morning for breakfast at home in Canada. My father remembers growing up eating it, as do I, and until my grandfather shared that story with me, no one really knew why we always had that meal for breakfast.

My Grandfather Today

It fills me with great sadness to say that, unfortunately, my grandfather passed away at the age of 94 in September of 2023. He was one of the very last remaining surviving Canadian soldiers from the war, and to this he dedicated his life. The Korean War did not end on the battlefield, and the horrors of combat stayed with my grandfather for a lifetime. He never forgot his fallen comrades and made sure to visit Korea every few years and pay respects at their place of rest. Despite this pain, his love for Korea and the people of Korea never faded. Although riddled with PTSD, he once told me that "even knowing everything that had happened, the trepidations, anxieties, and fears that were faced, I would do it all over again without question".

He donated thousands of dollars to build a monument in both Ottawa and Korea honoring fallen Canadian soldiers in Korea and Ottawa, ensuring their sacrifices were never forgotten. He loved speaking to students and educating them about Korea and the war. He proudly attended every Remembrance Day ceremony, memorial ceremonies and advocated for peace. In his final years, though cancer slowly claimed him, his spirit remained unbroken. Since his passing, he has been honoured in so many ways that are truly so special. My grandfather had so much love for the people of Korea, and they have so much love for him.

A Message for the Future Generation

The sacrifices of those who came before us were not free; all of the brave soldiers who fought in the Korean war sacrificed their futures to ensure that we can have one today. My grandfather and his fellow soldiers stood on the front lines fighting not for glory, but for the values of freedom, resilience, and unity. They endured unimaginable hardships so that others could live in peace. To the future generation: remember their sacrifice. It is our duty to preserve the history and legacy of the brave veterans' contributions, ensuring that future generations will remember and learn from their experiences as well. Even 72 years later, when you walk through Seoul and see the modern skyline and thriving economy, remember none of it would exist without the sacrifices made on those distant, blood-stained hills.

May we never forget the past, but carry it with us, always honoring those who served by shaping a future worthy of their sacrifice.

Flowers laid at the Canadian Memorial statue at the UNMCK in respects to Bernard Cote's passing (September 2023)

Bernard Cote with granddaughter Rachel Cote at the Remembrance Day Memorial in Windsor, Ontario, Canada (2022)

NEW ZEALAND

Period of participation	1950.08.01 ~ 1957.07.27	
Total number of troop deployments	5,322	
Ground Troops	Infantry battalion Forces	1 819 men
Navy	Frigate: 1	
Injuries of UN forces attended	KIA WIA POW Total	125 645 3 773

The monument of participation in the Korean War is located in Mokdong-ri, Buk-myeon, Gapyeong-gun, Gyeonggi-do

Echoes of Courage
My Grandfather's Legacy in the Korean War

In memory of Trevor Lynch
Written by Keishon R. Lynch

Trevor Lynch
16th Field Regiment Soldier

Keishon R. Lynch
University of Otago

About Me: A Grandson's Reflection

University Graduation Day, Dunedin, New Zealand (2023)

My name is Keishon Lynch, and I'm proud to have this opportunity to tell my grandfather's story. I have always been fascinated by history, international politics, and the legacy of war. Growing up, I was aware of my grandfather's service in the Korean War, but it wasn't until I pursued my studies in International Politics and War Theory that I truly came to understand the depth of his sacrifice and the significance of his experiences.

I have a Bachelor of Commerce in Business Management and a Graduate Diploma in International Politics from the University of Otago, New Zealand. I have spent years studying international security and foreign policy. These studies deepened my appreciation for how conflicts shape nations and how veterans like my grandfather played a direct role in securing the future we now enjoy. Without his dedication—both during the war and in the years of peacekeeping and rebuilding that followed—I wouldn't have had the same opportunities and outlook on life. His sacrifices paved the way for future generations, and his story continues to inspire me.

Visit to UNMCK, Busan (2023)

My passion for honouring his legacy has led me to South Korea twice as a Ministry of Patriots and Veterans Affairs/United Nations Youth Peace Ambassador, where I represented New Zealand and worked with fellow Korean War descendants to promote peace and friendship. During these visits, I saw firsthand the incredible transformation of Korea—a country my grandfather fought to protect.

Through my studies, my travels, and my involvement in veteran affairs, I aim to ensure that stories like my grandfather's are never forgotten. Trevor's story is the reason I plan on pursuing a career in diplomacy and peacekeeping.

New Zealand's Dedication to the Korean War

New Zealand played a significant role in the Korean War, demonstrating its commitment to international security as part of the United Nations coalition. When North Korea invaded South Korea on June 25, 1950, New Zealand was one of the first nations to respond. Under the UN flag, New Zealand sent 6 naval vessels and ground forces, contributing to South Korea's defense against communist aggression. One of the most

Meeting Judge Sang-Hyun Song, former President of the International Criminal Court and current President of UNICEF Korea(2023)

Korean War Memorial, Seoul(2024)

defining moments of New Zealand's involvement was the Battle of Kapyong in April 1951. This battle was a turning point in the war, as Chinese forces launched an overwhelming offensive against UN troops, attempting to break through to Seoul. The New Zealand 16th Field Artillery Regiment, where my grandfather, Trevor Lynch served, played a crucial role in holding the line and preventing the fall of South Korean positions.

The 16th Field Artillery Regiment, a unit of the New Zealand Artillery, provided essential fire support to Commonwealth troops, particularly the 3RAR [3rd Battalion, Royal Australian Regiment], and the 2PPCLI [2nd Battalion, Princess Patricia's Canadian Light Infantry]. As Chinese forces advanced in overwhelming numbers, the 16th Field Regiment rained down continuous artillery fire, effectively slowing enemy movements and preventing a breakthrough. Their precise and relentless bombardment became a key factor in the successful defense of Kapyong, forcing the Chinese to withdraw after suffering heavy losses.

For their actions, the units involved in the battle, including the 16th Field Regiment, were later awarded the United States Presidential Unit Citation, a rare and prestigious honour recognizing extraordinary heroism. The regiment's role in Kapyong not only saved countless lives, but also solidified New Zealand's reputation as a loyal and capable ally in global military operations.

16th Field Artillery Regiment in action, Battle of Kapyong
© Alexander Turnbull Library, Wellington, New Zealand.
Ref: K-0976-F

Kayforce departs from Wellington on December 10, 1950, aboard troopship SS Ormonde
© Alexander Turnbull Library, Wellington, New Zealand.
Ref: K-0123-F

While the armistice was signed in 1953, ending active hostilities, New Zealand troops remained in Korea as part of the post-war peacekeeping efforts. My grandfather, Trevor Lynch, was among those who stayed, serving until 1957. During this time, his unit helped maintain stability, supported reconstruction efforts, and ensured that South Korea remained secure in the fragile years following the war. His extended service highlights not only his personal dedication, but also New Zealand's long-standing commitment to international peacekeeping.

The bravery and sacrifices of New Zealand soldiers, including those of my grandfather and his comrades, remain a proud legacy, reminding us of the country's unwavering commitment to defending freedom on the world stage.

My Grandfather's Journey: Trevor Lynch's Service in Korea

When the Korean War broke out in 1950, New Zealand responded to United Nations' call for military support by forming Kayforce, which consisted of the 16th Field Regiment of artillery and ancillary units. Though the government sought 1,000

Trevor's Regiment in action (1951)

Speaking on behalf of all descendants of Korean Veterans to the Honourable Park Minshik(2023)

volunteers, nearly 6,000 stepped forward in the first month. Among them was my grandfather, Trevor Lynch, who was working as a junior accounts clerk at New Zealand's largest newspaper. Inspired by his family's military service—his father having fought in World War I and his two older brothers in World War II (one of whom was killed in action)—he felt it was his duty to serve.

Assigned to the New Zealand 16th Field Artillery Regiment, he trained for 12 weeks before departing Wellington on December 10, 1950. His regiment landed in Busan, South Korea, on New Year's Eve in 1950. What was meant to be a short tour turned into a seven-year service, making him one of the longest-serving New Zealand soldiers in the Korean War.

Trevor often spoke of the bitter cold—harsher than anything a New Zealander had ever experienced—and how deeply affected he was by the suffering of the Korean people.

Soon after arriving, his regiment moved north to the 38th Parallel, constantly wary of North Korean guerrilla activity. He took part in one of the most critical battles of the war—the Battle of Kapyong (April 22-25, 1951). This brutal conflict tested the Commonwealth forces—including New Zealand, Australia, and Canada—as they fought to stop a massive Chinese offensive. Trevor recalled staying awake for 48 hours straight, constantly watching for enemy breakthroughs. Despite being outnumbered, the Allied forces held their ground, preventing the fall of Kapyong, an achievement that later earned them a Presidential Unit Citation from South Korea.

One of his most haunting memories was surviving an artillery bombardment. His unit was miraculously spared when most shells overshot their position and landed in the next valley. When they advanced, they discovered that those shells had devastated an American battalion. The sights he saw that day stayed with him for life.

Later in the war, Trevor was wounded and hospitalised. Upon his return to duty, he was promoted to warrant officer and transferred to Regimental Headquarters in Busan. When the Armistice was signed in 1953, he remained in Korea, serving in post-war peacekeeping and rebuilding efforts. In 1954, he was transferred to Kayforce

Headquarters in Kure, Japan.

During his time in Busan, Trevor met Tsuruko, who later followed him to Japan when he was reassigned. They married in 1955, and in December 1956, they had their first child. He finally returned to New Zealand in 1957, with his wife and daughter following soon after.

Although he returned home, his connection to Korea never faded. For over 25 years, he returned annually, fostering ties with Korean War veterans, government officials, and the Korean Embassy in New Zealand. As the President of the New Zealand Korean War Veterans Association, he helped support Korean immigrants and continued strengthening New Zealand-Korea relations.

On each visit, he made sure to return to Kapyong, paying respects at the Kapyong War Memorial and contributing to scholarships for local high school students. He also ensured his three children travelled to Korea, passing on his deep respect for the country. His grandchildren, including myself, have continued this tradition, honoring his legacy.

For his dedicated service, Trevor Lynch was awarded several military decorations:

- Korea Medal (EIIR)
- United Nations Medal for Korea
- New Zealand Operational Service Medal
- Presidential Unit Citation (South Korea)

Trevor Lynch, Korean War Veteran(2006)

Despite the hardships, he always spoke of the meaning of his service. One of his most memorable quotes was:

"Many good men died for a good cause, and every time I see Korea's progress, I feel proud."

Trevor Lynch passed away in 2009, but his commitment to Korea never wavered. He often said that the Korean War was the most significant experience of his life—from the horrors of battle to the joy of witnessing Korea's post-war recovery. His dedication to peacekeeping and rebuilding Korea reflects the deep and lasting impact of his service.

Even today, his family continues to visit Korea, honouring his memory and ensuring his sacrifice and legacy live on.

A Message to Future Generations: Lessons from the Korean War

The Korean War is often called the "Forgotten War," yet its impact continues to shape our world today. For future generations, the war serves as a reminder of the cost of conflict, the importance of international cooperation, and the enduring struggle for peace. The sacrifices made by soldiers like my grandfather, Trevor Lynch, and his comrades in the 16th Field Regiment were not just about defending South Korea—they were about standing up for democratic values, protecting innocent lives, and maintaining global stability.

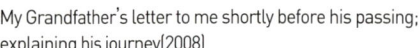

My Grandfather's letter to me shortly before his passing; explaining his journey(2008)

Han River Statue Unveiling - Representing peace and prosperity(2024)

The war left deep scars on both sides of the Korean Peninsula, with families torn apart and entire cities reduced to rubble. Yet, through resilience and determination, South Korea transformed itself into a prosperous and thriving nation. This remarkable recovery stands as a testament to what can be achieved when people refuse to let war define their future.

It also highlights the importance of continued diplomatic efforts to bring lasting peace to a still-divided Korea.

To younger generations, the Korean War offers valuable lessons. It teaches us the importance of remembering history—not just to honour those who served, but to learn from the past and prevent future conflicts. It also underscores the power of alliances and cooperation, as the war saw nations from around the world come together under the United Nations to fight for a common cause.

Perhaps most importantly, the Korean War reminds us that peace is never guaranteed—it must be protected, nurtured, and defended. My grandfather's service did not end when the fighting stopped; he remained in Korea until 1957 as part of the post-war peacekeeping efforts. His dedication, and that of countless others, shows that war does not simply end with a ceasefire—it requires ongoing commitment to reconciliation and stability.

As future generations inherit the world shaped by these past struggles, it is our responsibility to ensure that the sacrifices of those who served are never forgotten. By remembering their courage, learning from their experiences, and working towards a more peaceful future, we honour their legacy in the most meaningful way.

THAILAND

Period of participation	1950.11.07 ~ 1972.06	
Total number of troop deployments	6,326	
Ground Troops	Infantry battalion	1
	Forces	2,274 men
Navy	Frigates	3
	Transport Ship	1
Air Force	Transport formation flying unit	1
Injuries of UN forces attended	KIA	136
	WIA	1,139
	MIA	5
	Total	1,280

The monument of participation in the Korean War is located in Dongbaek-ri, Guseong-myeon, Yongin-si, Gyeonggi-do

Inheritance of Honor:
Memories and Values from My Grandfather's Service

In memory of Sakol Sritragool

Written by Wasita Sritragool

Sakol Sritragool
Lieutenant Colonel

Wasita Sritragool
Hankuk University of Foreign Studies

About Me

Hello, my name is Wasita Sritragool, the granddaughter of Sakol Sritragool, a Korean War veteran. I am originally from Thailand, and I have lived in Korea for 2.5 years during my graduate studies and right now, I am currently working in management team at a FMCG [fast-moving consumer goods] company in Thailand. I consider myself a friendly and outgoing person, which makes me enjoy meeting new people and participating in various activities. Furthermore, my aspiration to become a diplomat and deep curiosity about the world have profoundly shaped my life. From a young age, I envisioned studying abroad or participating in international programs as a representative of Thailand.

One day, by chance, I discovered valuable information about Thai veterans of the Korean War on my Facebook feed. Intrigued, I delved deeper into my research and discovered a wealth of valuable insights, particularly about the Youth Peace Camp. This experience broadened my perspective and introduced me to new opportunities that could guide my future path. Most importantly, I gained a profound understanding of peace as a foundation for stability and progress, fostering harmony and coexistence among people.

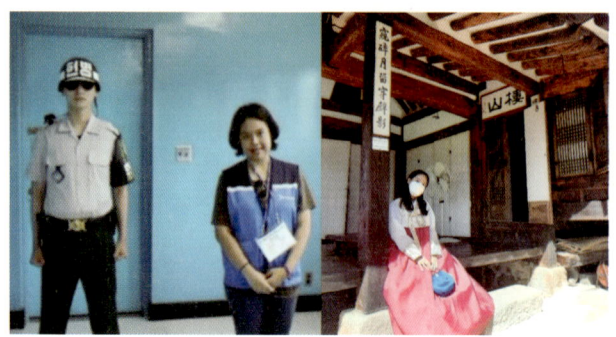

Learning about Korean culture with Uijeongbu Youth Student Center (2021)

Graduation Ceremony on February 16, 2024

The global rise of the K-Wave, particularly in the entertainment industry, has undeniably enhanced and elevated South Korea's international image. Beyond its cultural influence, South Korea boasts one of the most prestigious education systems in Asia. Given the cultural similarities between South Korea and Thailand, as well as the two nations' close geographical proximity, I developed a strong interest in pursuing my higher education there. After carefully exploring my options, I chose to pursue a master's degree in International Studies at Hankuk University of Foreign Studies with the support of various veterans' organizations. I graduated in 2024 and returned to my homeland to embark on the next chapter of my journey. Throughout this new phase of life, I carry with me the invaluable experiences and profound lessons gained during my time abroad. I will forever hold in my heart the brave warriors and the Republic of Korea, which has truly become a second home to me.

This opportunity allowed me to engage in a wide range of academic and professional experiences, including seminars, conferences, and collaborative programs organized by universities, private institutions, government agencies, and the embassies of both Thailand and South Korea.

Participating in many activities related to the Thai Embassy in Korea (2023)

Participating in a seminar on national peace with the descendants of war veterans (2022)

Thailand's Dedication

The Korean War was one of the most significant conflicts of the 20th century, marked by a confrontation between North and South Korea. Thailand was the first country in Southeast Asia to respond to the United Nations' call for military assistance in defending South Korea. Under the leadership of Field Marshal, Plaek Phibunsongkhram, the Thai government deployed the 21st Royal Thai Infantry Battalion, also known as the Thai Expeditionary Forces, to South Korea in 1950.[1]

Thai troops played a crucial role in several key battles. During the Battle of Bunker Hill, Thai soldiers played a significant role in defending key strategic positions. At Pork Chop Hill and along the Imjin River, they successfully secured and held frontline positions against repeated attacks by North Korean and Chinese forces during the Korean War. Their bravery and sacrifices were recognized by both the Thai and South

My grandfather at U.S. a Army base camp

My grandfather with a U.S. Air Force transport aircraft

---

1) Roy, D. (2003). Korean war and the United Nations' military involvement. Cambridge University Press.

Korean governments. After the war, many Thai veterans were honored with medals and decorations for their service.

Today, South Korea continues to maintain strong diplomatic ties with Thailand and expresses deep gratitude for the contributions of Thai soldiers. Thai veterans are regularly invited to commemorative ceremonies honoring those who fought in the Korean War, and memorials have been established to pay tribute to the Thai soldiers who lost their lives in the conflict.[2]

My Grandfather's Story

Cancer took my grandfather's life early in the morning on March 12, 2003, so I have always regretted having only nine years with him—just enough time for me to remember him with clarity. I grew up in a military family and lived in an extended

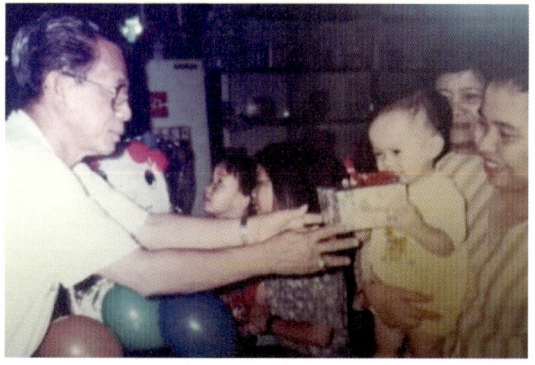

My first birthday party on March 3, 1997

---

2) Ministry of Foreign Affairs. (2020). Thailand-South Korea relations in the context of the Korean War. Ministry of Foreign Affairs Publishing.
Royal Thai Armed Forces. (2015). Records of the Korean War and the role of the Thai military. Royal Thai Armed Forces Headquarters.

family. Inside our home, on the walls of the living room, there were countless photographs of my grandfather from the time he served in various wars across different countries. Those images became a window into his past, allowing me to learn about his experiences through both the stories he told and the few questions I asked as a young child. From May 22, 1952, to January 31, 1953, my grandfather served in the Korean War under Rotation 6, the sixth Thai military contingent. He participated in the war as a Private and later retired from the army as a Lieutenant Colonel in 1989. My grandfather once shared that the greatest challenges for Thai soldiers during the Korean War were the harsh weather conditions and the scarcity of supplies. Additionally, Thai troops faced disadvantages in combat due to their smaller stature and fewer numbers compared to their opponents.

However, my grandfather explained that he was deployed during the later stages of the war, when the intensity of the conflict had begun to subside. As a result, he did not experience the full brutality of battle. Although war is an experience no one wishes for, my grandfather saw the Korean War as an opportunity for growth and learning. He worked alongside soldiers from various nations and witnessed firsthand the power of

My grandfather traveling to the Korean War aboard USS General H.W. Butner (AP-113)

The first time experiencing the coldest weather in his life

unity in achieving peace and stability. Furthermore, his experiences in the Korean War laid a crucial foundation for Thailand's later involvement in the Vietnam War, where Thai forces played a significant role and achieved notable success.

A Message to Future Relationships

Relationships are the essence of life, whether among friends, family, or loved ones. As we coexist in a world filled with diverse cultures, rules, and perspectives, the way we connect with one another becomes even more profound. Every relationship offers lessons and experiences that shape our growth, teaching us the value of understanding, resilience, and compassion. In the future, we will inevitably face challenges, transformations, and perhaps even the necessity of starting anew.

The world around us is evolving at an unprecedented pace. What once seemed distant and irrelevant can swiftly become a reality that affects us all. War, for instance, may appear to be a faraway concern, yet its consequences ripple across borders, touching lives both directly and indirectly. In war, there are no true victors—only loss, suffering, and wounds that time alone cannot heal.

Thus, I place my hope in the younger generation, believing that they hold the power to reshape our world. We must learn from the mistakes of the past, raise our voices for justice, and cultivate a society built on empathy and mutual understanding. The future rests in our hands. Let us choose peace over conflict, for peace begins in our minds, manifests in our words, and is realized through our actions.

GREECE

Period of participation	1950.12.09 ~ 1955.12	
Total number of troop deployments	4,992	
Ground Troops	Infantry battalion Forces	1 1,263 men
Air Force	Transport formation flying unit	1
Injuries of UN forces attended	KIA WIA POW Total	194 543 3 740

The monument of participation in the Korean War is located in Osan-ri, Ganam-myeon, Yoju-si, Gyeonggi-do

The Story of my Grandfather; a Korean War Veteran

In memory of Socrates Boutsikaris
Written by Socrates Boutsikaris

Socrates Boutsikaris
Greek Soldier

Socrates Boutsikaris
University of Veterinary Medicine Košice,
Slovakia

About Me

My name is Socrates Boutsikaris, and I am the grandson of a Korean War veteran. I am currently 21 years old and reside in Slovakia, where I am pursuing my studies at the University of Veterinary Medicine in Košice. I come from a family of three siblings. Coming from a family with a strong military background—both my grandfather and father having served—I grew up listening to stories about war and military life. As a young boy, I deeply admired my grandfather, who fought in two wars: the Korean War and the Greek Civil War. I was eager to learn as much as I could about his experiences. On one hand, my father shared his own knowledge of warfare with me; on the other, whenever I visited my grandfather, I would ask him about his time as a soldier.

Unfortunately, I lost my grandfather in 2013 when I was only nine years old. Now, at 21, I cannot put into words how much I wish he were still here so that we could have more mature conversations. The mere thought of sitting across from someone who endured years in the trenches of war, survived its horrors, and went on to raise a strong and loving family, fills me with admiration. The number of questions I have for him today is endless, as is the wisdom he could have passed down to me and my family.

In the summer of 2023, I had the incredible opportunity to visit South Korea as both

Attending Remembrance Ceremony for 70th Anniversary of the Korean War in Korea (2023)

Photo of my visit to the memorial cemetery of War Veterans in Busan (2023)

a family member of a war veteran and a representative of Greece. At last, I was able to see with my own eyes the places I had heard so many stories about and meet other veterans who had fought alongside my grandfather.

Walking through the streets of Seoul and Busan, I couldn't help but reflect on the sacrifices made by soldiers like my grandfather, Socrates. Without their courage and dedication, a peaceful and thriving South Korea might not exist today. This deeply emotional journey is something I will always carry in my heart, as it reinforced how meaningful and vital the cause he fought for truly was.

Greece in the Korean War

Greece's contribution to the Korean War was a powerful demonstration of its dedication to its UN allies. More specifically, Greece showed its unwavering support for the South Korean people by deploying 4,992 soldiers and seven Douglas C-47 Skytrain or Dakota, a military transport aircraft. This commitment was especially remarkable given that Greece had just emerged from the devastation of two consecutive wars—World War II (1939-1944) and the Greek Civil War (1946-1949). Despite its own struggles, Greece displayed extraordinary bravery and a steadfast commitment to the principles of freedom and international cooperation.

Greek soldiers in the Korean trenches
© mixanitouxronou.gr

The journey to Korea was arduous. The Greek soldiers endured a month-long voyage by sea, heading toward an unfamiliar land to fight in a war for a country most of them would never see again after the conflict ended. The psychological and emotional

"Lt. General Matthew B. Ridgway, U.S. 8th army commander, kisses the cross held by Chaplain Theofanis Tratolos, Greek Orthodox priest attached to the Greek battalion fighting in Korea, during the latter's celebration of Independence Day on the central front in Korea on March 31, 1951. Ridgway later reviewed the unit which has won an outstanding combat reputation while fighting with U.N. forces against the Reds."
© TheChaplainKit.com/greece

Korean War Anniversary Event, Greece (2010)

My grandfather getting his medal of honour (1971)

My grandfather getting his medal of honour in Korea (2006)

resilience required to face such an uncertain and brutal reality was immense.

Greek infantry played a crucial role in three key battles:

1. The Battle of Hill 381
2. The Battle of Outpost Harry – where Greek forces heroically defended their positions against overwhelming Chinese assaults
3. The Battles in Central Korea – where they engaged in fierce combat against Chinese communist forces

Military commanders praised the Greek contingent, stating, "The Greek forces distinguished themselves in battle, proving to be an invaluable asset to the division. Their steadfast defense at Outpost Harry remains one of the finest examples of courage in modern warfare."

My Grandfather's Story and Memories

My grandfather, Socrates Boutsikaris, was just 22 years old when he embarked on a long journey to Korea, joining the Greek forces in their mission abroad. During the 18 months he spent fighting for the freedom and independence of the Korean people, he endured immense hardships and witnessed the brutal realities of war.

Whenever I asked him to share stories from his time in Korea, he always recalled two in particular.

The first was about the unforgiving weather. He described the winter as the harshest he had ever experienced, often saying, "It felt like I was fighting in temperatures below -30°C. I couldn't feel my fingers for days." His account was not unique—at a veterans' gathering I attended years later, three other Greek soldiers echoed his memories, speaking of the extreme cold and the relentless winter conditions they had to endure.

The second story was about the fierce battle at Outpost Harry. He vividly remembered the chaos of combat, the treacherous terrain, and the sheer survival instinct that gripped every soldier on the battlefield. The horrors of war at this outpost left such a deep impression on my grandfather and his fellow infantrymen that they gave it a chilling new name: "Haros"—the Greek word for Death or the Reaper.

Message to the Future Generation

As a grandchild who bears my grandfather's name and carries his legacy, I consider it my duty to honor his memory and preserve the story of his bravery for future generations.

The Korean War is more than just a chapter in history—it stands as a testament to courage, resilience, and the sacrifices made in the pursuit of peace. To the younger generation, I urge you to honor this legacy by remembering the sacrifices of those who fought for this cause. To build a better future, we must remember the past and draw inspiration from those who endured immense hardships to provide us with the stability and peace we enjoy today.

SOUTH AFRICA

Period of participation	1950.11.16 ~ 1953.10	
Total number of troop deployments	826	
Air Force	Combat flying squadron	1
Injuries of UN forces attended	KIA POW Total	37 8 45

The monument of participation in the Korean War is located in Yongi-dong, Pyeongtaek, Gyeonggi-do

Alexis "Topper" van der Spuy:
My grandfather, My Hero, and a Hero of the Korean War

In memory of Alexis "Topper" van der Spuy

Written by Alessia Stefanutti

Alexis "Topper" van der Spuy
Fighter Pilot

Alessia Stefanutti
Durham University

About Me

Descendants trip to South Korea (2023)

Visiting the National War Memorial of Korea during the Descendants Youth Peace Camp (2023)

My name is Alessia, and I am currently living and studying at Durham University in the United Kingdom.

I am immensely proud to be the granddaughter of Alexis "Topper" van der Spuy, a South African fighter pilot who bravely served in the Korean War.

In the summer of 2023, I had the honour and privilege of travelling to South Korea to join the Descendants Youth Peace Camp. This journey deepened my understanding of a war so often referred to as "the forgotten war," and it reinforced how sincerely the people of South Korea appreciate and remember the sacrifices made by war veterans.

My grandfather passed away before I was born, but his legacy has always been a deep source of pride for my family. I felt a particularly close connection to him when I was in South Korea and I felt overwhelmingly proud, knowing how his bravery contributed to the freedom of such a beautiful country.

A moment that will stay with me forever happened while exploring the Gamcheon Culture Village in Busan with my team. We stopped at a food stall where I excitedly ordered my first Korean corn dog. When the vendor learned that we were the grandchildren of Korean war veterans, he insisted on gifting us the meal, as a gesture of gratitude to our grandparents. I was profoundly moved by this powerful and generous act, which embodied the gratitude and sincerity I witnessed throughout my time in South Korea.

I am deeply grateful to the South Korean government and the Ministry of Patriots and Veterans Affairs for giving me the opportunity to attend the Youth Peace Camp.

It was a life-changing experience that not only enlightened me, but also allowed me to forge lifelong friendships, whilst honouring my beloved grandfather. He, like so many others, travelled across the world to fight for South Korea's freedom.

South Africa's Dedication

South Africa was the first UN country to respond to the call for assistance in the Korean War.

On August 4, 1950, the Union Government announced it would send a squadron of fighter pilots and ground staff, calling on volunteers as it was not mandatory to serve abroad. By August 27, South African Air Force 2 Squadron, known as "The Flying Cheetahs," was brought to full wartime strength and prepared for deployment.

On November 16, 1950, the first South African pilots and ground crew arrived at the United States Air Force Base K-9 in Korea, operating under the U.S. Air Force's 18th Fighter Bomber Wing. Their missions included enemy strikes, ground support, reconnaissance, interdiction, and escort duties. Flying F-51 Mustangs and later F-86 Sabres, they completed 13,761 sorties, earning a reputation for their operational excellence, incredible skill, bravery, and dedication.

Trying Korean corn dog (2023)

Having fun with my friends I met on the Descendants Youth Peace Camp (2023)

A South African Air Force uniform on display in the National War Memorial of Korea in Seoul (2023)

My grandfather Topper van der Spuy (seated), with two of his fellow SAAF pilots (1951)

My grandfather Topper, a South African fighter pilot in Korea (1952)

However, their success came at a cost: 77 aircraft were lost, 34 pilots and two ground crew members were killed, one became a prisoner of war, and eight endured up to two years in captivity.

Although these courageous men made tremendous sacrifices, many South Africans remain unaware of their country's involvement in the Korean War and its crucial contribution to global freedom and security. It is essential that efforts persist to shed light on South Africa's role in this significant chapter of history, ensuring that the bravery and service of these great men is remembered and honoured for generations to come.

My Grandfather's Story

My grandfather, Lieutenant Alexis "Topper" van der Spuy, volunteered to go to Korea to fight for the freedom of the South Korean people. Topper was his wartime nickname.

A highly skilled South African fighter pilot, Topper had already earned recognition for his bravery and expertise during World War II. When the Korean War broke out, South Africa responded by sending an elite air force squadron of volunteer pilots, mechanics, engineers, as well as 2 Squadron South African Air Force, known as the "Flying Cheetahs." They joined forces with the U.S. Air Force 18th Fighter Bomber Squadron, proving to be an invaluable asset in multiple operations. Flying the formidable Mustang fighter aircraft, the squadron carried out reconnaissance missions, search-and-destroy operations, and numerous high-risk air sorties.

My grandfather arrived in South Korea in November 1951, and over the course of his service, he completed 67 combat missions. He led numerous successful strikes against enemy targets, often flying dangerously low to ensure precision and effectiveness.

Topper and his fellow SAAF airmen preparing to fly their Mustangs (1951)

My grandfather, Topper, loved animals. He befriended this little deer during the war (1951)

Beyond his exceptional skills as a pilot, Topper was loved by his squadron for his vibrant and jovial personality. Known for his ability to lift spirits, he would often play the guitar and sing to his fellow airmen, providing much-needed moments of fun amid the hardships of war. Many South African and American airmen who fought alongside him later recalled his presence in their memoirs, noting the lasting impact of his camaraderie and humour.

One of his most legendary days in the war was March 6, 1952, when he flew five combat missions in a single day. Targeting enemy vehicles, bridges, and hidden ammunition depots, he delivered devastating blows to opposition forces. However, during his fifth mission, his engine cut, causing the aircraft to lose power. Acting swiftly, he jettisoned his bombs, which exploded in the fields below, causing the bells of a nearby church to ring loudly. His Mustang crashed into a paddy field, and against all odds, he managed to escape the cockpit, drenched in fuel but grateful to be alive.

Rescued from the crash site, he returned to the American airbase, where he received a hero's welcome. In a moment of much-needed levity, the maintenance crew playfully hoisted him onto a small cherry-picker crane and paraded him through the main street of Wonju. As they passed through the village, children ran after the crane, cheering, waving, and laughing—an unforgettable scene that briefly brought laughter to a war-torn community.

Topper was well known for playing the guitar and singing to lift the spirits of fellow servicemen (1952)

Thankful to be alive after his Mustang crashed during his fifth mission of the day (March 6, 1952)

Having nearly reached the maximum number of allowable sorties for his tour, Topper flew just one more mission before his commanding officer, concerned that he was suffering with combat fatigue, ordered him back to South Africa. The American squadron gave him a memorable farewell party, celebrating not only a brilliant pilot, but also a dear friend.

My grandfather had a deep affection for the South Korean people and was willing to risk everything for their freedom. His immense courage, resilience, and kindness continue to inspire me, and I am very proud to share his story.

A Message to Future Generations

The Korean War is often called "The Forgotten War," yet its impact remains deeply remembered and felt to this day. The freedom and prosperity of South Korea today stand as a testament to the power of unity and the legacy of our forefathers' selflessness, courage, and sacrifice. Never let their stories fade. Keep their memories alive by learning, sharing and ensuring their contributions are never lost to time. Their courage shaped our history and it is our duty to preserve, respect, and honour their legacy.

Making memories and friendships for life at the Veteran Descendants Youth Peace Camp (2023)

BELGIUM

Period of participation	1951.01.13 ~ 1955.06	
Total number of troop deployments	3,498	
Ground Troops	Infantry battalion	1
	Forces	944 men
Injuries of UN forces attended	KIA	106
	WIA	336
	MIA	4
	POW	1
	Total	447

The monument of participation in the Korean War is located in Sanbongam-dong, Dongducheon-si, Gyeonggi-do

The Story of my Father,
Korean War Veteran Gustave Michel Sourbron

In memory of Gustave Michel Sourbron

Written by Lilianne Johanna Juliette Sourbron

Gustave Michel Sourbron
Sergeant 1st Class

Lilianne Sourbron

About Me

Me and my mother, I am 7 weeks old

I am Lilianne Sourbron and I was born on October 6,1956 at the Military Hospital B.S.D in Delbrück, Cologne, Germany. My father served in the Belgian army and was therefore stationed in Germany. I was my parents' first child.

A sister and three brothers came after me. Both my mother and father were from Belgium. My father was often away from home because of his participation in military exercises. I remember that he could be very strict, possibly because of the difficult childhood he had. However, I have more memories of my mother and sometimes say that she was the one who really raised us.

When my mother lived in Germany, she was very homesick for her native Belgium. I never felt completely at ease in Belgium, partly because houses in Germany tend to be more spacious and modern by comparison. As children, we almost always had our own bedroom there, which would not have been possible for us in Belgium at that time.

In Germany, I attended primary school. Then, from the age of 11 to 16, I followed a technical education in the Belgian town of Bilzen. I then worked in a sewing workshop and then at FN Zutendaal, where we made ammunition. After that, I worked in various warehouses where I collected customer orders, packed and prepared the orders for shipping, until my retirement in 2006.

At a young age, nineteen and unexpectedly pregnant, I married because I had to at the time. With my first husband, I had two children, a son and a daughter. After my divorce, I remarried a few years later in 2006, to my second husband. We had twins, a son and a daughter - every parent's dream.

My family picture

I worked from the age of sixteen until my retirement in 2016. Now I live in Munsterbilzen, Belgium, and the children have moved out of the house. From my eldest daughter, we have a grandson and granddaughter.

The Dedication of Belgium to the Korean War

The United Nations was deeply concerned about this war for fear that North Korea's attack on South Korea could turn into another world war.

In 1950, the Belgian government decided to respond to the UN's call to support South Korea. Through recruitment leaflets, men were asked to apply for the 'Belgian Volunteer Corps for Korea,' resulting in over 3,000 applications, of which 700 were eventually found suitable.

There were several reasons for their application: fighting communism, the desire for adventure, and good earnings. Many had never heard of Korea and did not even know where it was; for most, it was a journey into the unknown. They did not leave for Korea immediately. First, they underwent intensive training at a barracks in the Belgian town of Beverlo, near Leopoldsburg.

On September 13, 1950, the Belgian government pledged a 600-man volunteer battalion to support the UN in Korea, which arrived in January after three months of training.
© wikimedia.un.org

The ship Kamina leaves the port of Antwerp to Korea
© wikimedia.org

This training was quite tough: long marches and many exercises, both during the day and at night. To make it even more challenging, their rucksacks were sometimes filled with stones. During some exercises, sharp ammunition was even shot over their heads to force them to stay low to the ground.

The training concluded on the Parade Square in Leopoldsburg, where Prince Boudewijn, later King of Belgium, personally handed everyone the brown beret of the volunteer corps.

On December 18, 1950, the Belgian and Luxembourg soldiers of the 'Volunteer Corps Korea' departed from the port of Antwerp aboard the ship Kamina. This ship, originally a banana boat, had been converted into a troop ship.

Because it was a relatively small ship, many modifications had to be made to make it suitable for 700 soldiers. Some slept in beds that were sometimes arranged in three layers one above the other.

During the voyage, shooting drills were organised regularly to keep the military troops in top form. Despite everything, there was a good atmosphere on board, although it was extremely hot after passing through the Suez Canal. On January 21, 1951, the ship reached the South Korean port of Busan.

There, the men were placed under U.S. command. The battalion continued as the BUNC [Belgian United Nations Command].

Moreover, one of the platoons of this battalion was composed entirely of soldiers from the Grand Duchy of Luxembourg.

At that time, it was the middle of winter and bitterly cold, conditions the men were not initially prepared for. Once they had received suitable clothing to protect them from the cold, they left for the front near the Han River, about 20 kilometres from Seoul, on March 6, 1951.

Their task consisted of preparing and digging in positions and conducting patrols.

On March 18, 1951, platoon commander Lieutenant Pierre Beauprez stepped on a mine, becoming the first person killed in action in the Belgian Volunteer Corps in Korea.

In April, the men moved across the 38th parallel to Imjin, where they were attacked by large numbers of Chinese. In the attack, four Belgians were killed and more than thirty were wounded. The 2nd platoon suffered particularly badly there.

The battalion commanded awe and respect from Allied troops. For the bravery of these soldiers from both Belgium and Luxembourg, the battalion was awarded six honorary awards including one American and one Korean.

Heavy losses were suffered during the deployment of the Volunteer Corps Korea between 1950 and 1953, with 106 Belgian and two Luxembourg soldiers killed and more than 300 wounded. Four Belgian soldiers are still missing.

A total of 3,498 Volunteer Corps soldiers left for Korea. Many of them left twice, some even three times. The last volunteers returned to Belgium in July 1955.

The following entries are affixed to the banner of the Belgian Order of Leopold:
- IMJIN: Battle of Imjin from April 22-26, 1951. Awarded on January 4, 1952.
- HAKTANG-NI: Battles from October 9-13, 1951. Awarded on June 25, 1953.
- CHATKOL: Battles from March to April 1953. Awarded on July 22, 1953.
- COREE-KOREA: From January 31, 1951 to July 27, 1953. Awarded on January 14, 1954.

The following honourable mentions were also awarded for the battle of Imjin:
- US award: Presidential Unit Citation, awarded on September 6, 1952.
- South Korean award: South Korean Presidential Unit Citations, conferred on June 7, 1952.

The gold-coloured Cross of Honour for Military Merit was added to the banner by the government of the Grand Duchy of Luxembourg on May 27, 1994.

My Father's Story

My father was born on July 3, 1928, in Liège, Belgium. He was the eldest of three children, including two younger sisters. His childhood was difficult due to his father's absence from the family. As a result, my father had to be the sole breadwinner for the family at a very young age.

World War II brought additional complications. My father was only twelve of age when the war broke out. While working on the farm, he fell through the attic and seriously injured his knee, requiring a long stay in hospital. Despite his mother's objections, he was approved for Korea and enlisted in the 'Volunteer Corps Korea.' His motivation was gratitude for the liberation of Belgium by the Americans at the end of World War II.

After his training in Beverlo, Belgium, near Leopoldsburg, he left for Korea on December 18, 1950, on the ship 'A957 Kamina'. He served as a private and was assigned to C-Company.

About his time in Korea, where he went twice, he told little. What I did know from him was that it was extremely cold on arrival, with temperatures dropping to minus 20 degrees at times, heavy snowfall, and harsh conditions caused by frozen, rock-hard mud.

In March 1951, he was moved to the Han River for patrols and in April 1951, he

Gustave Michel Sourbron

Gustave Sourbron at the 38th parallel, the border between North and South Korea

found himself in the attack of thousands of Chinese near the Imjin River. He said there was no direct support from the Americans then, as only the Belgians were there. He then had to do something he found terrible: flee and leave behind four fallen Belgian soldiers. In April, his battalion moved across the 38th parallel to North Korea. There too, the men found themselves in fierce firefights with the Chinese.

When he returned to Belgium on October 1, 1951, he met Marie Thérèse Hansen and began a relationship with her. Having previously re-enlisted for the Korean War, he left for the front again on June 10, 1952. It is clear that the fighting had once again become intense, as shown by the following commendation he received from the Belgian Ministry of Defense:

"As squad commander of the line-layers, in Korea, in the service of the United Nations, he distinguished himself particularly during the fierce and victorious battles fought at Chatkol in March-April 1953, against a challenging and fanatical enemy, namely during the attack of 18 to 19 April and led his squad under fierce bombardments, with remarkable coolness and devotion to duty."

After his return in 1955, he married Thérèse, and together they had five children—two daughters and three sons.

Wedding picture

The Luxembourg and Belgium Korean War Memorial, located in Dongducheon-si, Gyeonggi-do, South Korea, commemorates their participation in the Korean War. ©wikimedia.org

On his final return, he, along with Dutch veterans, landed in the Netherlands by plane. A small delegation of government and defence representatives stood ready to present awards only to the Dutch. So the Belgians stood there empty-handed. Immediately afterwards, he returned to Belgium, where it was only after some time that he received the recognition he deserved for his efforts during the Korean War. He received several awards related to the Korean War, such as the United Nations Service Medal, Korean War Medal, Korean Presidential Unit Citation, American President Unit Citation, and many others.

On December 23, 1999, 18 veterans of the Korean War, including Gustave Sourbron, received a special medal: the honourable mark of two crossed swords, in recognition of their heroic deeds during the war in Korea from 1950 to 1953.

Gustave Sourbron remembered vividly what happened. He could talk about it sometimes, but he still got very quiet when he thought back to the misery he experienced at the front. During an interview, he said, "In March '51, we were on patrol in the no man's land, as they call it. That's the part of the front line between the enemy and us. We were under attack. It was terrible... My best comrade, someone I had met during training, was killed. Horrible... I can assure anyone that when you are stuck with each other for so long, a very close bond develops. It was broken just like that. And I couldn't have done anything about it. I had to leave his body, along with those of many others. We had to flee and that stays with you forever."

He became a professional soldier after returning to Belgium and ended his military career as a sergeant 1st class on January 1, 1975.

After retirement, he was active as a board member of several organizations and dedicated himself to Belgian Korean War veterans. On June 17, 1986, he received a certificate of appreciation from the Korea Belgian Veterans Association like the picture below:

Korean War veteran Gustave Sourbron passed away on February 12, 2002, in Bilzen, Belgium. His wife, Marie-Thérèse Hansen, followed on February 17, 2025, also in Bilzen.

A Message to the Future Relationship

My father's efforts were not in vain. He was proud of his contribution to the liberation of South Korea. Although he never returned to the country where he fought after the war, he kept both positive and negative memories of that time.

The bond with his allies always remained strong. This contains an important message: in this troubled world, it is crucial that people remain committed to our values and standards, even if it involves personal risk. Every soldier, including those in our Belgian army, understands the importance of such a mission.

Upon their return, Korean War veterans hardly received any appreciation or recognition for their efforts. Let us not repeat this mistake and make sure that our future soldiers—those who protect us and help others—are properly honored and appreciated for their service. Gratitude should not wait for anniversaries or ceremonies; it must be active, visible, and enduring. It is our solemn duty to remember the sacrifices of our veterans and to preserve the historical truth of their service, for a nation that forgets those who defended its freedom risks losing the very values for which they fought.

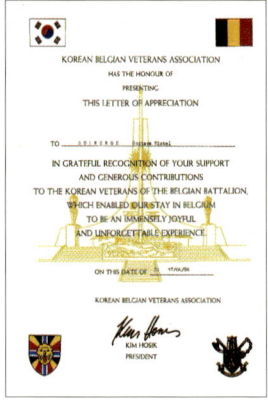

Cerificate of Appreciation KBVA

The Belgian Volunteer Corps, including Gustave Michel Sourbron

PHILIPPINES

Period of participation	1950.09.19 ~ 1955.05	
Total number of troop deployments	7,420	
Ground Troops	Infantry battalion combat team Forces	1 1,496 men
Injuries of UN forces attended	KIA WIA MIA POW Total	112 299 16 41 468

The monument of participation in the Korean War is located in Gwansan-dong, Dugyang-gu, Goyang-si, Gyeonggi-do

A Legacy of Kapwa between the Philippines and Korea

In memory of Martin Dalingay Sr.
Written by Mary Ellen Burro

Martin Dalingay Sr.
Master Sergeant

Mary Ellen Burro
Hankuk University of Foreign Studies

About Me

Master's Degree Graduation at HUFS Minerva Hall (February 2025)

My name is Mary Ellen Burro, but in Korea, I go by 장유미 (Jang Yumi). Though born and raised in the Philippines, my journey and identity extend beyond its shores, into the heart of Korea—a country my grandfather, MSgt. Martin Dalingay Sr., once fought to protect. In February 2025, I completed my master's degree in International Development at Hankuk University of Foreign Studies. But this achievement isn't just about education; it's part of a deeper connection to a land that has always been intertwined with my family's history. It is the place where my grandfather's sacrifices continue to echo, and where I first began to truly understand his story.

Growing up, I heard fragments about my grandfather, a Filipino soldier who fought in the Korean War. He passed away before I was born, but his legacy was a shadow that loomed over our family, a name spoken with a mix of pride, reverence, and quiet sorrow. I knew he had been part of the PEFTOK [Philippine Expeditionary Force to Korea], a group of brave Filipino soldiers who answered the call when North Korea invaded the South. I knew he had fought in a war that wasn't ours, and that when he came back home, he wasn't quite the same. But as a child, the depth of his experiences and the toll it had on him were not something I fully understood.

It was only after I moved to Korea that I began to feel the weight of his legacy—one that had been passed down through whispered stories and unspoken memories. I realized that his life was intricately tied to this country in ways I had never imagined.

The War My Grandfather Brought Home

The stories I grew up hearing about my grandfather were fragmentary, like pieces of a puzzle that I could never fully complete. He never spoke much about the war. Perhaps it was because it was too painful, or perhaps it was the generational silence that often accompanies trauma. My mother remembers that when she was young, he would hum Arirang, the hauntingly beautiful Korean folk song, around the house. She didn't understand its significance at the time. It was just a tune, a song from a faraway land. But years later, when I first heard the same song in Korea, I realized that it was more than just a melody. It was a song of loss, of longing, a silent tribute to a place and people my grandfather had fought for but could never fully forget.

I often wonder if that song carried with it the memories of the friends he lost, the battles he fought, or perhaps the part of himself that he left behind in Korea. But he never spoke of it, and neither did anyone else in my family. Instead, the stories came through my mother's fragmented recollections of his quiet moments—how he would look at old photos of soldiers, his eyes distant as though he were seeing something no one else could.

After living in Korea for a while, I came to understand that these memories were not unique to my grandfather. Many soldiers who fought in the Korean War carried their experiences with them in silence, unable to speak of the horrors they had witnessed. For my grandfather, it wasn't just the physical scars he brought back—it was the invisible wounds. I began to suspect that he had PTSD, a condition that was not recognized or treated in his time. The signs were subtle, and it was never confirmed, but the stories I heard—how he would sometimes break into fits of rage for no clear reason, how he would often withdraw into his thoughts, distant and unapproachable—made me think that the war never truly ended for him.

The Philippines and Korea: A Bond Forged in War

The Filipino soldiers who fought in the Korean War were part of something much larger than themselves. The Philippine government sent troops to support South Korea under the banner of the United Nations, following North Korea's invasion of the South in 1950. It was a conflict that neither the Philippines nor Korea had initiated, but one that they would share nonetheless. The Philippines wasn't just fighting for another nation's freedom; they were standing side by side with their Korean brothers and sisters in arms.

For the Philippines, this wasn't just a military action; it was a reflection of kapwa— a core Filipino value that transcends national borders. Kapwa is the idea that we are all connected, that the suffering of others is our own, and that we should stand together in times of struggle. When the Philippines answered the call to defend South Korea, it was more than an act of international diplomacy. It was a recognition of shared humanity.

In this light, the Filipino soldiers didn't see themselves as strangers on foreign soil. They saw themselves as part of a larger family, standing shoulder to shoulder with the Koreans they were helping. It wasn't just about fighting in a war—it was about forging a bond that would last for generations. My grandfather, though he never spoke of it,

Retired Martin Dalingay Sr.

Martin Dalingay Sr. (right) with his friend (left) when they first joined the military

carried this sense of kapwa with him. He fought not only for the freedom of the Korean people, but for the promise of shared dignity and shared humanity. The bond between the Philippines and Korea, though not widely known or celebrated in the Philippines, is one of sacrifice, unity, and mutual respect.

During the war, the Filipino soldiers fought in some of the most intense and grueling battles, including the Battle of Yultong, where they held their ground against overwhelming Chinese forces, and the Battle of Hill Eerie, a fight where the Filipino soldiers endured fierce trench warfare. Despite the brutal conditions, Filipino soldiers endured, driven by a sense of duty and the spirit of kapwa.

When the war finally ended in 1953 with the signing of the armistice, the soldiers returned home, but they brought the war with them. While South Korea rebuilt and honored the sacrifices of its veterans, many Filipino soldiers like my grandfather returned to a country that had moved on, with no formal recognition or acknowledgment of the pain they carried.

The Price of Sacrifice

My grandmother often spoke about how, after the war, my grandfather seemed different. He had seen too much, witnessed too many horrors that he couldn't leave behind. He had come home physically, but emotionally, part of him had stayed in Korea. My mother recalls how, at times, he would slip into long silences, staring at nothing in particular, lost in a world that no one else could understand.

The signs of trauma were there, but no one knew how to address them. The concept of PTSD wasn't understood back then, and certainly not in the Philippines. The military, too, offered no support for the invisible scars that soldiers carried with them. My grandfather, like many others, simply had to endure. He didn't receive counseling or care; he had to cope with his experiences in the best way he knew how—by burying them deep inside. His struggles were never openly discussed, but it was clear from the stories passed down to me that he had been deeply affected.

Years later, as I walked through the War Memorial of Korea, the weight of my grandfather's experience truly hit me. As I stood before the memorial, I traced my fingers over the engraved names of Filipino soldiers who had fought alongside their Korean counterparts. They were there, etched in stone, remembered by a country that understood the significance of their sacrifice. It made me feel both pride and sorrow—pride for their bravery, but sorrow for the lack of recognition they received back home in the Philippines.

Walking in My Grandfather's Footsteps

Living in Korea, immersing myself in its history, its people, and its culture, I began to feel a deep connection to this land. It wasn't just a place where I was studying; it was a place where my grandfather had once walked. I began to understand the war through a different lens—not just as a historical event, but as something personal. My grandfather's footsteps were the same as mine, though separated by decades. The streets he walked on were now familiar to me, and the stories he carried with him were slowly unfolding in my mind.

As I learned about Korea's rise from the ashes of war, about its transformation into the thriving, modern country it is today, I realized how deeply intertwined our histories were. My grandfather had fought for the future of a nation he would never fully see, and yet his sacrifice had helped shape the future of not just South Korea, but the Philippines as well. It was a legacy of sacrifice, honor, and solidarity that I now carry with me every day.

The Responsibility of Remembrance

Though my grandfather never asked for recognition, and though his sacrifices were largely forgotten in the Philippines, I have made it my mission to remember. The story of Filipino soldiers in the Korean War is one that deserves to be told, and it is a story that must not be lost to time. The Philippines' role in the Korean War is often overlooked, but the truth is that many Filipino soldiers gave their lives defending a country they had never known, a country that would go on to flourish, while they returned to lives marked by quiet hardship with their sacrifices echoing through the years, often unrecognized.

As a Filipino, it is my responsibility to honor my grandfather's sacrifice and to share the story of the kapwa bond between the Philippines and Korea. In doing so, I hope to honor not only the soldiers who fought, but also the generations that followed—the ones who stand as living proof that the spirit of kapwa transcends borders, time, and conflict.

Though my grandfather's war was not mine, his legacy lives within me, and it lives it lives within all of us. As I continue my journey, I will carry his memory forward, never allowing his sacrifices to be forgotten. It is not just a family legacy; it is a shared legacy of two nations that will always be connected by the blood and sacrifice of those who came before us.

Wearing Hanbok outside the palace during my summer vacation in Korea (2023)

Continuing the Legacy:
Writing the Next Chapter of the Story

In memory of Francisco P. Encomienda
Written by Joon Shin Encomienda Amangan

Francisco P. Encomienda
Master Sergeant

Joon Shin Encomienda Amangan
Kookmin University

About Me

Joon Shin Encomienda Amangan in South Korea (2024)

My name is Joon Shin Encomienda Amangan, and I am a citizen of the Republic of the Philippines. I submit this article in honor of my late grandfather, Master Sergeant (MSgt) Francisco P. Encomienda, a veteran of the Korean War.

At the time of this writing, I am residing in Seoul, South Korea, where I have been pursuing a Master's degree in Sociocultural Psychology at Kookmin University since 2023. In addition to my academic pursuits, I currently serve as Chairman of the AYNK [ASEAN Youth Network in Korea], a student organization operating under the auspices of the AKC [ASEAN-Korea Centre]. This organization is dedicated to fostering and strengthening relations between ASEAN member states and the Republic of Korea. Consequently, beyond my familial connection to the Korean War, I have established a further link to Korea through my involvement with AYNK.

This dual connection has afforded me the privilege of being selected as one of the descendants of veteran soldiers from the sixteen nations that contributed troops to the United Nations Forces during the Korean War, to share the narratives of our respective grandfathers. It is essential to emphasize, however, that this narrative is not centered upon myself, but rather upon the life of MSgt Encomienda. This document serves as a biographical account of his experiences before, during, and after the Korean War.

A Friendship from Even Before the War

I will begin by highlighting the enduring alliance between my country, the Republic of the Philippines, and the Republic of Korea. Our nations share a poignant history, particularly the shared experience of Japanese colonial rule. While the Philippines endured three years of Japanese occupation, Korea experienced a longer period of 35 years under Japanese colonial rule. Following the defeat of Japan by the United Nations forces, both countries achieved independence. The Philippines declared its independence in 1946, while South Korea was established in 1948.

Given the shared experience of U.S. support in their respective paths to independence, the establishment of diplomatic relations between the Philippines and Korea was a natural progression. Notably, the Philippines was the fifth country in the world—and the first in Southeast Asia—to officially recognize the Republic of Korea. This bilateral relationship was formally solidified on March 4, 1949, marking the inception of an enduring alliance that continues to flourish today.

The seeds of the Philippine-South Korean alliance were sown during the Korean War. Despite the Philippines' then state of recovering from Japanese colonial rule, the decision to send troops to support South Korea was a natural consequence of the existing bond between the two nations.

At the outbreak of the Korean War, General Carlos Romulo, then President of the fourth session of the United Nations General Assembly, played a pivotal role in securing UN intervention. As a prominent Filipino general, Romulo strongly advocated for the provision of military aid to South Korea. His impassioned plea ultimately led to the Security Council Resolution 83, which authorized military action from the UN forces in the Korean Peninsula.

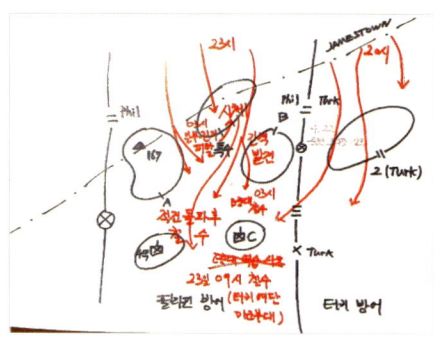

The Battle of Yultong's Tactical Deployment (1951)
"율동전투-07" by 조현우9930, © 2020

In response, President Elpidio Quirino, then Commander-in-Chief of the Philippine Government, announced the mobilization of Filipino forces to aid South Korea and the United Nations Forces. A nationwide call to arms was issued, inspiring a surge of volunteers from young Filipino soldiers. This swift mobilization made the Philippines the third UN member state and the first Asian nation to assist South Korea, resulting in the formation of the PEFTOK [Philippine Expeditionary Forces to Korea]. PEFTOK was recognized for its efforts in various battles during the Korean War. However, the most notable contribution of PEFTOK in the Korean War occurred in the Battle of Yultong (율동전투).

The Battle of Yultong unfolded on April 22, 1951, in the northern part of Yeoncheon County, Gyeonggi Province, South Korea. Facing a formidable Chinese force of 40,000 troops, the 10th BCT [Battalion Combat Team] of PEFTOK, a determined force of 900 men, valiantly defended its position. Despite being heavily outnumbered, the Filipino soldiers fought with unwavering determination, repulsing numerous enemy assaults and inflicting heavy casualties on the Chinese. This fierce resistance played a crucial role in halting the Chinese Spring Offensive, stabilizing the UN front lines. Moreover, this remarkable Filipino victory thwarted the Chinese ambition for a decisive victory, which would have potentially led to the complete conquest of the Republic of Korea and the collapse of the United Nations Command.

The Hero of the Story

My late grandfather, MSgt Francisco Panganiban Encomienda, was born on July 24, 1932, in Cuyapo, Nueva Ecija, in the Philippines. Raised on a farm, he excelled academically, consistently achieving honor roll status. One day, he was just playing checkers with his friends when news came out about an ongoing military recruitment. Despite his parents' disapproval, he embarked on a journey to Manila, leaving behind the familiar comforts of home, to enlist in the military.

MSgt Francisco P. Encomienda (1952)

At the young age of 20, driven by a sense of duty and a desire to make his family proud, he answered the call to serve his country. He first enlisted in the Philippine Army, but transferred to the Philippine Air Force, where he was subsequently assigned to the 19th BCT of PEFTOK. My grandfather, along with the platoon he belonged to under the 19th BCT, was deployed to Korea in 1952. This distinguished unit earned the honor of being the first PEFTOK battalion to receive the South Korean Presidential Distinguished Unit Citation, a testament to their valor. They were also recognized with a Battle Citation from the US X Corps.

His specialization as a soldier was in radio technology. Therefore, his main role was to operate radio equipment to communicate with surrounding allied forces. He also went to the battlefield alongside the rest of his platoon, placing him on the front lines during the Korean War.

Fortunately, he returned to the Philippines after the Korean War without sustaining significant injuries. He continued his military service and later married my late grandmother, Beatriz Gavina Encomienda, in 1965. They were blessed with two children: my mother and my uncle. Over the years, their family grew, and they were eventually blessed with nine grandchildren.

His unwavering dedication to his country as a soldier spanned over three decades, culminating in his retirement as a Major Sergeant in 1982 at the age of 52—a testament

My grandfather's platoon during the Korean War (1952)

My grandfather in South Korea (1953)

to the bravery he displayed on that fateful day he answered the call to duty.

Though my memories of my grandfather are a bit hazy as I was very young when he was alive, I vividly recall him frequently tinkering with a large radio in his room. This recollection makes perfect sense considering his role as a radio technician during the Korean War, where he was responsible for critical communication between allied forces. His expertise also brought the NATO Phonetic Alphabet and Morse Code into the lives of every member of the family. I remember fondly engaging in friendly competitions with my siblings, testing our knowledge of these codes and seeing who could recall all the codes for each letter of the alphabet.

Even in his later years, my grandfather maintained a consistent routine, waking up before sunrise. He would regularly visit the bakery early in the morning to fetch fresh pan de sal (salt bread) for us and prepare a simple breakfast of eggs and hotdogs to accompany it. It's funny that I still remember how he often burnt them, but we still enjoyed eating them because

Encomienda family (1979)

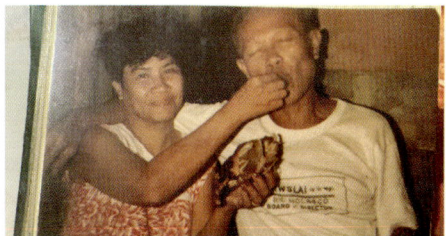
My grandfather with my grandmother (1995)

Three generations of the Encomienda family (2005)

the skin would become crispy and toasted. While not overly expressive, it was through these small acts of care that he silently expressed his deep love for his family. However, it was in the kitchen, the very heart of his love for his family, that tragedy struck. While preparing breakfast, hot oil spilled on his legs, leading to health complications that ultimately resulted in his passing.

My grandfather lived a long life of 77 years. He passed away on January 17, 2009, and was buried in the Libingan ng mga Bayani, roughly translated as "Cemetery of the Heroes", in Taguig, Philippines.

Continuing the Legacy

Stories of great individuals often leave us asking: What comes after the hero is gone? I believe the greatest tribute is to live with the same courage and purpose they once carried—to embody that same heroic spirit. In my family, we felt a profound sense of responsibility to carry on the work my grandfather started. We understood that we

My grandfather's gravestone (2010)

My uncle in Syria (2012)

needed to step up and continue where his story left off.

The first to follow in my grandfather's footsteps was my uncle. He enlisted in the Philippine Air Force, just as his father had done before him. As a soldier, he also had the opportunity to contribute to peace efforts, serving as a member of the UNDOF [United Nations Disengagement Observer Force] in the Golan Heights, Syria from 2011 to 2012. He continued to serve his country until his retirement in 2022.

On the other hand, my mother dedicated herself to supporting the families of PEFTOK veterans by serving as one of the directors in the PVAI [PEFTOK Veterans Association Inc.]. Now, she focuses on guiding and inspiring the grandchildren of these veterans to carry forward the living legacy their grandfathers brought to life.

Likewise, my younger brother, inspired by the valor or of his grandfather and uncle, recently enlisted as a soldier in the Philippine Air Force, bravely stepping forward to continue the family's proud tradition of service.

As for me, I am currently pursuing a Master's degree in Sociocultural Psychology in South Korea. Beyond my academic pursuits, I actively share my grandfather's story, inspiring young people with his service during the Korean War through public talks and youth programs. Moreover, I've had the privilege of connecting with other

PVAI Emblem (2018)

My mother in South Korea (2024)

grandchildren of Korean War veterans here in South Korea, individuals who, like myself, are utilizing their voices and positions to create a positive impact on their communities.

Using Our Own Talents for a Better Tomorrow

My grandfather enlisted as a soldier driven by a desire for peace, believing he could contribute by serving on the front lines. My uncle and my younger brother, inspired by his example, followed in his footsteps and also chose to serve in the military. As for my mother, she dedicated herself to supporting the families of war veterans, while also inspiring and educating their grandchildren. This demonstrates that there are many ways to contribute to peace and a better future, each of us utilizing our unique talents and strengths.

Driven by a strong academic aptitude and a desire to contribute to a more peaceful world, I am pursuing my studies in Korea with the goal of becoming a researcher specializing in multicultural families. I've witnessed firsthand how intermarriages,

Sharing my grandfather's story in South Korea (2024)

such as those between Filipinos and Japanese, can bridge cultural divides. Initially, some families may harbor historical resentments, but the presence of mixed-race grandchildren often softens these tensions, gradually eroding intergenerational animosity. I firmly believe that these multicultural families play a vital role in building a more peaceful and interconnected world.

We are all unique individuals, endowed with diverse talents and interests. We share a common aspiration: to utilize these gifts to create a better world for future generations. My grandfather's sacrifice during the Korean War, enacted over half a century ago, remains a powerful inspiration. We continue to benefit from his service, enjoying the peace and security he helped secure. Therefore, I urge each of us to cultivate our talents and dedicate them to the betterment of society. Let us live with a guiding question: 'How do I want my descendants to remember me?' My grandfather's actions, performed long ago, demonstrate the enduring impact of our present deeds. Even seemingly small actions can have a profound ripple effect on future generations. As his descendant, I am filled with pride in his contribution to a noble cause.

Let us all live with our descendants in mind. Their pride will be our lasting legacy, a testament to our contributions that no one can diminish.

Türkiye

Period of participation	1950.10.19 ~ 1971.06	
Total number of troop deployments	21,212	
Ground Troops	Infantry brigade Forces	1 5,455 men
Injuries of UN forces attended	KIA WIA POW Total	900 1,155 244 2,299

The monument of participation in the Korean War is located in Dongbaek-ri, Guseong-myeon, Yongin-si, Gyeonggi-do

My Grandfather's Past, My Future with Republic of Korea

In memory of Sadık Asımgil

Written by Ilayda Asımgil

Sadık Asımgil
Turkish Soldier

Ilayda Asımgil
Hankuk University of Foreign Studies

About Me

My name is Ilayda Asımgil, and I am a proud descendant of a Turkish Korean War veteran. Though I was born long after the war ended, the stories and sacrifices from that time have always felt close to my heart. As someone who grew up hearing about the Korean War and its impact, I've come to understand how deeply those experiences shaped not only my ancestor's life, but also mine in ways that continue to unfold even today.

Now living in Korea myself, working as a cultural bridge between Germany, Türkiye and Korea, I feel an even deeper connection to this country and its people. Through my work in media, public events, and international relations, I've had the privilege of exploring how the past shapes the present and how remembrance can spark understanding between generations and across cultures.

This book is more than just a historical account. It's a personal journey—a tribute to the veteran in my family and a reflection on how their courage and sacrifice continue to live on through the lives of their descendants. I hope that by sharing this story, others will also be reminded of the strength that can be passed down through memory, love, and legacy. We will always remember.

The Proud Story of My Grandfather During the Korean War

My Grandfather during the 2002 World Cup Korea/Japan in Jamsil Sport Complex

In 1950, more than 5,000 soldiers gathered in the Turkish port city of İskenderun to embark on a 22-day journey to Busan, South Korea. Their families saw them off with faces filled with sorrow and concern while the soldiers themselves displayed a mix of determination and excitement. This scene, much like a scene from a film, describes the moment my grandfather, Sadık Asımgil, left home. Born in 1929 in Mersin, Türkiye, he was serving as a private in İskenderun when his unit was ordered to support South Korea against North Korea.

The Korean War started on June 25, 1950, and ended with a ceasefire on July 27, 1953. More than four million people lost their lives. Türkiye was the second country, after the United States, to dispatch troops in response to a UN Security Council resolution calling for aid to South Korea. Among the Turkish soldiers who answered this call was my grandfather.

As for my parents, they eventually settled in Germany, where they have lived for over 30 years. Every summer, our family visited relatives in Mersin, a city in Türkiye, where my grandfather eagerly awaited us. He would always tell us stories from the Korean War and his time as a soldier. He often said, "I can never forget that country. I still dream about my time in Korea. The people there are full of warmth, and their way of thinking is similar to ours." In 2002, he had the opportunity to revisit Korea for eight days in commemoration of the FIFA World Cup. He was deeply moved by the modern and advanced nation Korea had become and felt immense pride in the decision he had made half a century earlier to fight there. My grandfather passed away in 2014, but his stories laid the foundation for my deep interest in Korea.

A Wartime Episode from 1950

My grandfather's diary contains an account of the battle at Geumyangjang-ri (now Gimnyangjang-dong, Cheoin-gu, Yongin). This battle took place on January 26, 1951, when overwhelming Chinese forces clashed with the Turkish brigade. In his diary, he wrote:

"In the mountains and forests, we exchanged gunfire with Chinese soldiers. My comrades and I tried to track the direction of the bullets to determine the enemy's position. We crouched in fear, dodging the relentless gunfire. At one point, while adjusting my helmet, a bullet ricocheted off it

and struck my superior officer's hand. Had I not been adjusting my helmet then, my life would have ended there. I quickly wrapped my officer's hand in cloth. Later, with the help of American air support, we destroyed enemy vehicles and advanced through the bombed wasteland. Upon reaching Pyongyang, I witnessed the brutal and devastating consequences of war."

Despite the horrors of war, my grandfather also had fond memories. A music lover, he often played tunes for his fellow soldiers, earning the nickname "the mood maker." Korean War veteran Mahomet mentioned him in his diary, writing:

"On December 31, 1950, as we welcomed the New Year, I found a rare moment of happiness. We ate turkey at our camp while listening to Sadık Asımgil's music. That was a true moment of joy."

Reading these words, I could vividly imagine the scene.

My First Encounter with Korea and My First Steps

Parties were always a highlight of Turkish family gatherings. My grandfather played

My Grandfather in Mersin, Türkiye (2003)

My Grandfather Sadık Asımgil (1950)

the flute, my father played the hand drum, and my mother, younger sister, and I danced. These moments are memories I cherish deeply.

In 2018, I visited Seoul for the first time. Before my trip, my uncle told me that my grandfather's photograph was displayed at the War Memorial of Korea in Yongsan. With pride and curiosity, I went there in April 2018. In the exhibit dedicated to NATO allies, I saw the words, "Türkiye, the blood brother nation."

When I found my grandfather's photo and newspaper articles about him, I couldn't hold back my tears. At that moment, a museum guide was explaining the contributions of Turkish soldiers to Korean visitors. I pointed to my grandfather's picture and proudly said in Korean, "That's my grandfather." Hearing this, the visitors clapped and shook my hand, thanking me. I will never forget that moment.

Thanks to my grandfather, I formed a deep connection with Korea. His sacrifice and dedication inspired me to learn Korean, understand its culture, and make Korea a part of my life. Though far from my homeland, Korea feels close to my heart.

My Life in Korea

Five years have passed since I took my first steps in Korea. Over the years, I have grown both personally and professionally, working in YouTube content creation, broadcasting, and event coordination—all while actively pursuing my aspirations. As a graduate student at Hankuk University of Foreign Studies, I study International Relations with a scholarship and work as a freelancer.

In May 2023, my parents visited Korea for the first time through the program "My Neighbor, Charles." Seeing their tears at my grandfather's photo at the War Memorial and the graves of Turkish soldiers at the UN Memorial Cemetery in Busan was a deeply moving experience. My parents told me that my work in Korea made them proud and that my grandfather would be proud of me as well.

Following My Grandfather's Footsteps

I actively participate in programs that invite Korean War veterans and their descendants back to Korea. Seeing these veterans' pride and emotions when witnessing Korea's transformation is a priceless experience. I also help organize camps for the descendants of Korean War veterans, giving them a chance to visit South Korea, the country their ancestors fought for.

As I walk the paths my grandfather once did, I feel a deep sense of responsibility to keep his memory alive. My mission is to ensure that the sacrifices of Korean War veterans, including my grandfather, are never forgotten.

My Future Goals

I want to share the story of my grandfather and South Korea with the world, which is why I chose to study International Relations. Many young people today are unaware of the struggles Korea endured to become the nation it is today. As the saying goes, "A nation that forgets its history has no future." Through broadcasting and storytelling, I aim to honor my grandfather's legacy.

Living alone in a foreign country has been challenging, but I have grown stronger. I hope to continue developing myself and positively influencing others.

"My Neighbor Charles" KBS TV program (2023)

Youtube shooting for Arirang TV (2024)

A Letter to My Grandfather

Dear Grandfather,

Even though you are no longer with us, you are always in my heart. I am in Korea thanks to you. I miss you more than words can express. There are so many things I wish I could ask you. If we could walk hand in hand along the beach, I would share all my dreams with you. But even though you are not physically here, I know you are watching over me from above. I love you, and I will never forget your sacrifice.

Your granddaughter, Ilayda Asımgil

National ceremony for the Korean War UN Veterans Day on July 27, 2022, in Seoul

Korean War Veterans Descendants Camp (2023)

Sodaemun Prison History Hall Memorial ceremony host (2024)

Korean War Veteran Revisit Program (2022)

A Stone of Memory, A Pillar of Friendship: The Story of Ahmet Şahna, "Koreli Ahmet

In memory of Ahmet Şahna

Written by Eren Yıldırım

Ahmet Şahna
Medic Corporal

Eren Yıldırım
Sungkyunkwan University

About Me

On the 100th Anniversary of the Republic of Türkiye Reception in Seoul (2023)

My name is Eren Yıldırım. I am currently pursuing a Ph.D. in Political Science and Diplomacy at Sungkyunkwan University. Beyond my academic journey in pursuit of knowledge, I am also striving to preserve one of my family's most cherished legacies: the memories of my grandfather, Ahmet Şahna, from the Korean War.

Forged by Hardship: The Early Life of Ahmet Şahna

My grandfather was a Turkish soldier who left a lasting impact with his courage and sacrifice, fighting thousands of kilometers away from his homeland to become a beacon of hope for another nation. His story is not just that of a soldier, but also of a young boy who grew up in hardship, a young man who struggled to survive, and a warrior whose character was forged on the battlefield.

Ahmet Şahna was born in 1932 in Yusufeli, a secluded town nestled in the mountains of Artvin, a province overlooking the turbulent waters of the Black Sea in Türkiye. Life

The Membership Card of Ahmet Şahna in the Association of Veterans of the Korean War (1970)

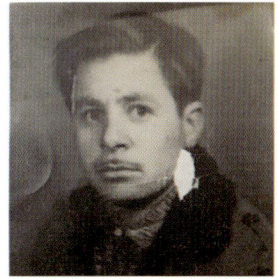
Ahmet Şahna's Youth Years (1958)

revealed its harsh face to him at an early age. His family had been displaced from lands that once belonged to the Ottoman Empire by the Russian forces.

At just five years old, he lost his father. The burden of responsibility that fell on his small shoulders became one of the most defining forces that shaped his character. Growing up without a father made him disciplined, self-reliant, and hardworking. While other children played in the streets without any responsibility, he had to learn how to stand firm against life's challenges.

By the age of fifteen, he was already working in a lumber factory in a distant town, far from his village. With his small frame, he dragged massive logs from one place to another. The weight of the work was relentless, sometimes merging with the exhaustion that seeped into his bones and the hunger that gnawed at his stomach. But giving up was never an option for him. He worked to survive and support his family. Every weekend, he walked nearly 20 kilometers each way to visit his mother, returning to his village on foot, and setting off again Monday morning. This resilience, gained at such a young age, would later become his greatest asset on the battlefield. His childhood and youth were overshadowed by poverty, but he never wavered. Every hardship taught him patience, perseverance, and the strength found in adversity.

The Weight of Determination: Ahmet Şahna's Journey to Korea

One day, while flipping through an old newspaper, his eyes caught a headline: "The Korean War Breaks Out." Below the headline, there was a black-and-white photograph of women and children fleeing in despair. A deep sadness filled his heart. Memories of his own difficult childhood flashed before his eyes—hunger, suffering, and loss. He saw his own past in those desperate faces. Overwhelmed with emotion, he made a decision at that very moment: he had to join the Korean War. Soon after, news spread that Türkiye would be sending troops to Korea. Ahmet rushed to the recruitment office without hesitation. He gathered the necessary documents for voluntary enlistment and stood in line for his medical examination, his heart pounding with excitement at the opportunity he had been waiting for. When his name was called, he stepped forward eagerly. The doctor, without even beginning the examination, gave him a long, scrutinizing look. Then, putting down his pen, he asked in a voice filled with compassion: "Son, why do you want to go to Korea?"

Ahmet's throat tightened. He had so much to say, but words felt insufficient. He could only utter, "For the innocent children..." The doctor studied the young man standing before him. Though his thin silhouette bore the weight of years of hardship, his eyes held an unyielding fire. Yet, reality could not be ignored—Ahmet weighed only 48 kilograms. The doctor shook his head and said, "I cannot enlist you, son. You're too underweight." Ahmet felt as if a heavy stone had been placed on his chest. A boy who had learned how to struggle through life did not know how to give up. Without losing the fire in his eyes, he locked eyes with the doctor and said, "Commander, I want this mission more than anything. Give me time, and I will reach the required weight." A brief silence filled the room. The military officers, impressed by the young man's determination, exchanged glances. One of them turned to him and said, "I'll give you six months to reach at least 55 kilograms. Then we'll see if you can be enlisted!"

This was yet another battle for Ahmet—but he had never backed down from a challenge.

A photo taken as a memory just before the military service in Korea (1952)

From that moment on, his only goal was to gain weight and go to Korea. He ate excessively for months, forcing himself to consume more than he ever had before. Even while working, he carried food in his hands. Slowly, his body gained strength, replacing years of fatigue with newfound energy. At the end of six months, he proudly stood before his commander, weighing 58 kilograms, and gave a crisp military salute.

For the rest of his life, he recounted that moment with a proud smile: "Those six months were the only time in my life I ate so much!" And thus, his journey to Korea began. He embarked on a long train journey across Türkiye, bidding farewell to his homeland. As the train rattled along the tracks, he reflected on the life he was leaving behind and the uncertain future ahead. But the real challenge was yet to come: a 30-day voyage across the ocean. As the ship groaned under the weight of the waves, his heart swelled with anticipation. Finally, the ship reached Busan Port. The moment his feet touched Korean soil, an indescribable feeling washed over him. It was not just another battlefield—it was the place where his destiny would change forever.

A photo from the Turkish-Korean Friendship Night that Ahmet Şahna attended in Korea

As a medic corporal, Ahmet's duty was not only to fight, but also to save lives. The first sights of Korea were haunting: devastated cities, collapsed homes, and children wandering the streets with fear in their eyes. But he met this reality not with sorrow, but with a soldier's discipline and a sense of duty. He knew emotions alone would not change anything—he had to take action.

Through countless nights, he worked tirelessly to heal wounded soldiers. Every injury tested his endurance, every life saved became a silent victory. His commanders and fellow soldiers admired his dedication, courage, and unwavering spirit. In emergency moments, Ahmet understood that the war was not just about military strategy or territorial battles; it was about preserving the dignity of those who had lost everything, offering a hand to those who had no one left to turn to. In his eyes, Korea was not just another battlefield. It became a second home, a place where his footprints remained in the snow and his memories were carried by the wind. It was where he gave his strength, his compassion, and a part of his soul.

Beyond the Battlefield: Ahmet Şahna's Lasting Connection to Korea

As Ahmet witnessed the suffering of the Korean people, a deep bond formed in his heart. The historical ties between Turks and Koreans had existed for centuries, but the Korean War solidified their brotherhood. Even after he returned to Türkiye, that bond never faded. Everyone knew him as "Koreli Ahmet," meaning "Ahmet, the Korean" in Turkish. Whenever he met another Korean War veteran, his eyes were filled with tears and he embraced them with longing. He was very sensitive about receiving a veteran's pension and never accepted any financial offer related to the Korean War throughout his life. He repeatedly emphasized that Korea and the war were the matters of honor, dignity, and pride to him, and that even if he were starving, he would never accept such money.

In 2002, he received an official invitation from the Korean government to attend the World Cup in Korea. He cherished the letter so much that he kept it by his bedside for months. However, time had prepared another test for him. Alzheimer's disease slowly began to erase the memories from his mind. He started to forget even his wife, his children, and his grandchildren. But strangely enough, he never forgot Korea or its people. As he spoke about Busan's port, the streets of Seoul, and the battlefields he had witnessed, his eyes still sparkled like in the old days. He even remembered the taste of the rice he ate in Korea. He recalled the devastation caused by the war, the fear on the faces of the children back then; but at the same time, he watched Korea's development over the years on television with pride. If he had ever been able to visit Korea again, he would have wanted to walk peacefully through the streets where soldiers once took photographs on the battlefield. But his illness did not allow him to fulfill this wish. On August 4, 2015, Ahmet Şahna passed away, leaving behind a legacy of sacrifice, courage, and deep bonds of friendship.

In the last years of his life, Ahmet Şahna shared his days with his life companion, Asiye Şahna (2011)

What We Can Learn from 'Koreli' Ahmet: Notes for the Future

In 2018, when I was selected as a recipient of a Turkish government scholarship to study in Korea, I made a vow to fulfill my grandfather's final wish and internalize the importance of peace rather than sanctifying a war. Before I came to Korea, I brought a small stone from his grave and have since traveled across this peaceful and prosperous land, sharing his story and honoring his memory. I hope this stone strengthens the bond of brotherhood between Türkiye and Korea and reinforces peace in both our countries. For us, Korea represents the bond of brotherhood, one born from sacrifice and mutual respect among those who gave their lives for the land. Ahmet Şahna's memory and sacrifice will forever remain a symbol of the everlasting friendship between Türkiye and Korea. If you ever visit Türkiye, remember that you have brothers and sisters there waiting to welcome you.

Ahmet Şahna's story is more than a soldier's sacrifice; it is a profound lesson in courage, perseverance, and humanity. Though he grew up in poverty, Ahmet's determination to bring hope to strangers highlights the strength of belief and resilience.

A stone taken from Ahmet Şahna's grave now travels through Korea, the country he wished to see after the Korean War but never had the chance to visit. (2018)

It serves as an inspiration for both Turkish and Korean youth, showing how the lessons of the past can shape the future.

The presence of thousands of Turkish soldiers in Korea during the war symbolizes a shared destiny and unbreakable bond—a friendship born in war and carried forward as a lasting legacy. Ahmet Şahna and countless other unsung heroes were not just soldiers carrying weapons; they were compassionate and courageous individuals who upheld their humanity even in the darkest times. It reminds us that true heroism lies not in conflict, but in the pursuit of peace. The fact that my grandfather never forgot Korea, even as his illness progressed, and continued to speak of his deep connection to that distant land, is a powerful expression of sacrifice and loyalty.

People say wars are fought for national interests, yet it's people who suffer the consequences of a war—ordinary men and women caught in violence, chaos, fear, and a deep desire for peace. Ahmet Şahna did not see Korea as a foreign land, nor did he see Koreans as strangers. He saw them as human beings suffering, struggling, hoping, just like his own people. My grandfather knew that the silent acts of kindness and sacrifices would be remembered far longer than the battles themselves. From him, we can learn that the future must not be built on hatred or vengeance, but on understanding and hope, elevating the spirit of those who chose compassion amidst chaos.

From Turkey and Korea's relationship, we can see that although nations may be

A photo series of Ahmet Şahna, spanning from his later years to his middle age (2007, 1989, and 1967).

divided by language, race, and borders, brotherhood transcends all. We honor those who endured war to teach us the true cost of conflict and the lasting importance of peace. We commemorate all the soldiers who strived to let the next generation live in a country where one's liberty is protected.

As the generation that owes our peace to our ancestors, let us carry with us this lesson: to preserve and fight for peace within ourselves, our country, and our world. In the words of Mustafa Kemal Atatürk, the founder of the Republic of Türkiye: "Peace at home, peace in the world!" (국내에서의 평화, 세계의 평화!).

May the souls of Ahmet Şahna and all the heroes who gave their lives in the Korean War rest in peace.

The compilation of these cherished memories would not have been possible without the invaluable contributions of Ahmet Şahna's beloved wife, Asiye Şahna; his children, Refika Yıldırım, Bilge Şahna, and Ergün Şahna; and his grandchildren. With heartfelt gratitude, I extend my deepest thanks to them all.

LUXEMBOURG

Period of participation	1951.01.31~ 1953.01	
Total number of troop deployments	100	
Ground Troops	Infantry platoon	1
	Troops	48 men
Injuries of UN forces attended	KIA	2
	WIA	13
	Total	15

The monument of participation in the Korean War is located in San 48, Sangbongam-dong, Dongducheon-si, Gyeonggi-do

The Diary-Writing Soldier, Jean Stoffel

In memory of Jean Stoffel

Written by Max Stoffel

Jean Stoffel
Reserve Lieutenant

Max Stoffel
Secretary-Coordinator of the
Luxembourg-Korean Association

About Me

My name is Max Stoffel, the youngest son of Jean Stoffel, a Korean War veteran. I live in the Grand Duchy of Luxembourg in Gasperich, a district of the country's capital. Korea was a distant country for me as a child and the only thing I knew was that my father had volunteered there.

Unfortunately, he died in 1973 when I was only 7, but I still remember him well. However, he rarely talked about his mission in Korea.

My interest in his period as a volunteer from 1950 to 1951 only began in 2011, when a team from the Luxembourgish military museum contacted me to make a documentary film about the 100 Luxembourgers who volunteered to help the Korean people. On that occasion, I was given documentation with decorations, mission reports written by my father, and some photos of him. Then, when my mother passed away in 2014, we found his diary, medals, and lots of photos of his time in Korea while clearing out her house.

In 2021, I was contacted by the Director of our National Museum of Military History to provide them with information about my father, as he and his team were in the process of preparing a major exhibition on the volunteers of the Korean War.

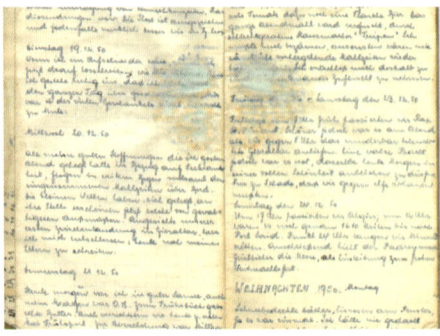

A diary my father wrote during the war

Seeing my father on a giant screen during the ceremony; very emotional moment! (September 2023)

THE STORY OF UN KOREAN WAR VETERANS

Given my profession as a teacher, my thirst for more information grew, so I plunged into the adventure of finding out more about his mission and Korea itself.

I have now spent over a year with my diary project. The beta version of my father's war diary is now ready to become a real book. In fact, I have managed to turn it into a 200-page document with all the moments my father wrote down in his little notebook day by day from December 18, 1950, to September 30, 1951; all in four languages (French, English, German, and Korean) with maps and photos. This diary is intended to revive the experiences of a volunteer soldier to honour my father with a personal memorial which is important to me. 100 Luxembourg volunteers fought for Korea's freedom and this willingness must not be forgotten. It is a memorial to the volunteers who bravely went to distant lands to fulfil their duty in a brutal war between two opposing ideologies, and at the same time shows how important it is to preserve the voices of those who witnessed history from the heart of the action. A digital version of it will also be available soon.

A great first adventure for me was the opportunity to attend the ROK Army's 75th anniversary celebrations in September 2023 in Seoul. The Revisit Korea Program is also on my bucket list.

Luxembourg and the Korean War

As the first major clash of the Cold War, the Korean conflict (1950-1953) forced the Grand Duchy of Luxembourg to position itself clearly on the international political scene. Together with Belgium, it provided a detachment of fighters within the framework of a UN mission and thus made a firm commitment to the American ally and the "free world". All 100 Luxembourgish soldiers were volunteers!

Two infantry platoons of Luxembourg participated from

At the War Memorial Museum (September 2023)

September 1, 1950 to January 31, 1953 in this mission. The first contingent (September 1950 to September 1951) consisted of 43 volunteers: 22 civilians, and 21 soldiers. The second contingent (January 1952 to January 1953) consisted of 46 volunteers: 12 civilians, and 34 soldiers.

Finally, a total of 100 Luxembourgish volunteers contributed to the War effort in Korea. 2 soldiers were killed and 13 wounded in action.

The number of 100 soldiers may not seem like many, but you have to remember that in 1950 Luxembourg didn't even have 300,000 inhabitants, with an army of around 3,000 soldiers.

I really do not know exactly why my father embarked on this risky adventure. In any case, it is important to know that, both he and his brothers-in-arms, spent part of their youth under German occupation during the World War II. Thus, they all knew very well what it meant to be invaded by a neighboring country and to suffer all the consequences of it. From 1940 to 1945, Luxembourgers lived in fear and suffering.

In 1950, when it came to helping Korea against its invader, the Luxembourg government did not want to commit its newly created army immediately, so it called on volunteer soldiers, as it had previously. More than 350 men turned up, and in the end 85 were declared fit. The two contingents were therefore ready.

My Father's Story

My father with other soldiers (October 1950)

As mentioned earlier, I can only speculate as to the true reason why my father embarked on this risky venture. However, I believe it was partly due to a falling out with his parents and partly driven by a genuine desire to help.

Fortunately, throughout his mission, he kept

a little diary in which he wrote down day by day some impressions of his experience.

Here are a few quotes:

Thursday, 21 December 1950 (on the boat "Kamina" from 18.12.1950-31.01.1951)

I was in a good mood this morning, and my stomach was okay, too. We had real butter for breakfast. We also did our first-morning exercise today. For a change, the lunchtime soup was burnt and was served with a raw tomato as a side vegetable, as well as with a bottle of beer. The whole evening meal was spoilt by poorly made home-made "Treipen" Black pudding (not the British version!)

I had to control myself, otherwise all the meals would have come back up.

I, therefore, decided to take comfort in a tin of pineapple.

Sunday, 18 March 1951 (battle near the Han River)

Received the sad news of the death of Lt Beaupré? who, together with an American captain, sergeant and lieutenant Verhagen, ran into mines on the other side of the Han River. Nothing at all was found of the American sergeant and only a few pieces of the captain and lieutenant.

Monday, 23 April 1951 (Imjin)

Le grand cirque (The big circus)

Around 9.30 a.m. we started, everything ready. C Company shot the first Chinese who [had] come within a few metres of their positions. At 10 o'clock the racket started and continued until A Company ran out of ammunition. The bridge we [had] crossed (over the Imjin) *had been occupied by the Chinese, so there was no question of retreating. At 6 a.m. a reconnaissance party left our position with the objective: bridge. Some of them came back. Chief Frank went with a reconnaissance party to C Company to increase its firepower, as it had suffered many losses. Then a column made its way through the Chinese lines to bring ammunition to C Company. This gave them the opportunity to retreat. The whole operation took place without aircraft and tank support, as these were more urgently needed elsewhere. Jabs [fighter-bombers] and two* motorised Invaders only arrived in the late morning hours. While they worked on the Chinese, who in the meantime had occupied the positions of C Company, we prepared to retreat. We only took the most important material with us because we had to wade through the Imjin. Enemy mortar fire increased in intensity. The last ones in our positions blew everything up. Tents, kitchen facilities, dental equipment, several tonnes of ammunition, huge piles of C rations and all the Bergems (large backpacks), trailers, cars, etc. My flute was also blown up on this occasion. The cars fought their way through the Chinese, supported by tanks. The co-drivers fired all they could. - We walked about 10 kilometres, heavily loaded and with wet feet, and were then loaded onto lorries and driven out of the danger zone.

After returning from Korea, my father hoped to rejoin the Luxembourg Army. However, like other soldiers who had served in Korea—known as "brown berets" because they had worn brown headgear during their mission with the BUNC [Belgian UN Corps]—he faced difficulties. These veterans, proud of their nickname, were often seen as outsiders or adventurers, and some higher-ranking officers in the Luxembourg Army didn't welcome them back.

As a result, my father enrolled in a military school in Belgium. After some time, he was able to return to the Luxembourg forces, this time as a reserve officer. In that role, he was stationed in Bitbourg, Germany, and later at the Walferdange barracks in Luxembourg.

Watching over the land at an observation post (1951)

A little break with a Korean child behind my father (1951)

Giving information to the rest of the platoon (1951)

In 1954, he left the army and got married on August 23 of the same year and the couple had three children, of whom I was the youngest, born in 1966.

My father began his career as a civil servant in the Luxembourg government, first in the Ministry of Transport, where he was in charge of driving licenses. Then, in the early 1970s, he joined the Ministry of Finance. Unfortunately, he developed angina pectoris and suffered a fatal heart attack on August 23, 1973. He passed away on his 19th wedding anniversary, leaving behind his wife and three young children.

My Life Today

Having gathered valuable information and stories over the past few years, I have decided to take a more active role in the veterans' organization here in Luxembourg. In addition to my job as a teacher, I now serve as the secretary-coordinator of the Luxembourg-Korean Association, a voluntary role that gives me a great deal of satisfaction. Our association is making every effort to ensure that this so-called 'Forgotten War' is remembered, so that our dear veterans are never forgotten.

When I retire in 2026, I plan to return to Korea to retrace the route that my father took in February 1951 from Busan to Seoul.

My Personal Message to the Readers

The Koreans are great and loving people who are full of gratitude and sympathy. They still show their appreciation for the help they received. Their remarkable recovery has shown the world how vital it is to remember history and how a country can rise again like a phoenix from the ashes, like they did after the war, thanks to the steadfast support of many allied nations. My deepest respect for this country, its culture, and its people!

COLOMBIA

Period of participation	1951.05.08 ~ 1955.10	
Total number of troop deployments	5,100	
Ground Troops	Infantry battalion	1
	Forces	1,068 men
Navy	Frigate	1
Injuries of UN forces attended	KIA	213
	WIA	448
	POW	28
	Total	689

The monument of participation in the Korean War is located in Gajeong-dong, Seo-gu, Incheon

From Cali to Seoul:
Carrying My Grandfather's Legacy

In memory of Santiago Gaona Cadena

Written by Stephanie Arguello Gaona

Santiago Gaona Cadena
Corporal

Stephanie Arguello Gaona
Sookmyung Women's University

About Me

Stephanie Arguello. Yongin-South Korea. Peace Camp (2022)

My name is Stephanie Arguello Gaona, I'm from Cali, Colombia and I've been living in Korea for almost 8 years now.

My first connection to Korea was both accidental and transformative. In 2007, I stumbled upon a Korean drama, Witch Yoo Hee, that captured my imagination. At the time, I knew little about Korea, but the glimpse it offered into its unique culture and traditions intrigued me.

My curiosity deepened when my father handed me a book titled "Enough with Latin American Excuses," which critiqued development models and highlighted Korea's astonishing transformation after the war.

This was more than just an academic interest—it became a personal mission. Could Colombia learn from Korea's development model? Could the resilience and determination that rebuilt Korea inspire a change in my home country? These questions sparked a journey that would eventually lead me to Korea.

Stephanie Arguello. Korean War Memorial Park, Seoul-South Korea (2022)

Stephanie Arguello. ADB Korea tourism trip (2024)

While studying Political Science in Colombia, I observed Korea's rising global influence and its growing ties with my country. Access to information about Korea became easier and my academic focus increasingly centered on this remarkable nation. Then, as I planned my move to Korea, an eye-opening family revelation changed everything.

I sought my grandfather's support to fund my studies. That's when he shared something I had never known—he had fought in the Korean War. His stories of courage, hardship, and unwavering determination gave me a deeper connection to Korea. Suddenly, this wasn't just about a country I admired from afar; it was about a shared legacy and a personal mission to honor his sacrifices.

After years of saving money and working tirelessly, I finally arrived in Korea. Now, as a graduate student studying International Cooperation for Development, I immerse myself in the lessons of Korea's "Miracle of the Han River." Living here has been transformative, helping me grow academically and personally, and reaffirming my commitment to building bridges between Colombia and Korea.

Colombia in the Korean War

Colombia's involvement in the Korean War is a powerful testament to solidarity and courage. As the only Latin American country to send combat troops to Korea, Colombia made a bold and historic contribution to the United Nations coalition. Between 1951 and 1954, 5,100 Colombian soldiers served alongside forces from the United States and other allied nations.

The journey was not an easy one. These young men, most of whom had never left their country, traveled thousands of miles to a foreign land they knew none about. They endured extreme conditions, from Korea's harsh winters to the intensity of frontline battles. Yet, they faced these challenges with remarkable resilience and determination.

Colombian troops were involved in several key battles, including the famous Battle of Old Baldy and the Battle of Hill 400. Their bravery in these confrontations earned them respect and admiration from their allies. Major General Bryan Blackshear once remarked, "I have fought in three wars. I thought there was nothing left for me to see in the field of heroism and human intrepidity; but I needed to see the Colombia Battalion fight."

The sacrifices of the Colombian soldiers extended beyond the battlefield. They faced the psychological toll of war, the challenges of adapting to an unfamiliar culture, and the loss of comrades. Despite this, their commitment never wavered. Their efforts laid the foundation for a lasting bond between Colombia and Korea, one built on shared sacrifice and mutual respect.

Today, this bond continues to grow. The legacy of Colombia's participation in the Korean War is a source of pride for both nations and is a living example of international cooperation in times of crisis.

On December 26, 1950, the Colombian Battalion was created to participate in the Korean War, as a demonstration of the Colombian government's anti-communist policy. Colombia was the only Latin American country that sent troops to the Korean War © wikimedia.org

My Grandfather's Story and Memories

My grandfather, Santiago Gaona Cadena, was only 16 years old when he embarked on a 30-days journey by ship to Korea in 1951. With just four months since he had joined the Army, he volunteered to join the "Battalion Colombia" in the Korean War. In his own words, when asked why he decided to volunteer, he said, "I'm not sure why; I didn't even think it twice. Maybe because of my youth—my adventurous desire of wanting to know more places. I don't know. And also, my drive to protect the weak. In my mind, at that time, Korea was the weakest country."

Shortly after his arrival to Korea, he turned 17, making him one of the youngest members of the Colombian contingent. His experiences in Korea were marked by extraordinary challenges and profound moments of courage. "We were kids—we liked to goof around, we loved to play, we were not yet those warriors that you see in movies," he said.

One of the most harrowing battles he participated in was the Battle of Kimhwa Hill 400 in June 1952. Company A of the 3rd platoon launched a surprise attack on the Communist's outpost located 500m north of the allied forces at dawn and captured the Hill. It then destroyed the enemy's strongly built defense facilities before returning. He vividly recalls the chaos of combat, the loss of comrades, and the sheer determination of the Colombian Battalion to succeed. He recalls, "There was nothing harder than saying goodbye to a friend, not because the friend was going back to Colombia, but because he was going to the cemetery… I had to say goodbye to 163 friends, comrades, brothers". Despite immense challenges, their efforts helped American forces push forward, a testament to their bravery and

Santiago Gaona In Busan (1951)

Santiago Gaona – Korean War Memorial Park, Seoul, South Korea (September 2019)

Santiago Gaona. Project Soldier. Courtyard by Marriot Time Square. Seoul, South Korea (September 2019)

resilience. After a successful operation, his contingent, Company A of the 3rd platoon, was granted 15 days of leave, and to this day, he recalls it as one of his greatest joys. "We were about to get some money, so we could buy things in the store. Sergeants called out names one by one to hand us the money, but they didn't call mine. I started asking for my name, so did everyone else, yet, my name was not on the list as I had been promoted from private to corporal," he said.

The physical conditions were equally grueling. My grandfather often described the bitter Korean winters, which were unlike anything he had ever experienced. Without proper clothing, he endured freezing temperatures that made even basic movements difficult. However, he recalled that in the midst of the chaos, Koreans lifted everyone's spirits by singing "Arirang," a traditional Korean folk song, and eventually, most of the soldiers learned the song and joined in like a beautiful choir.

In August 1952, during a night patrol, his vehicle was struck by a grenade, leaving him seriously injured.

He narrowly avoided losing his leg and was sent back to Colombia later that year. Despite the pain and trauma, he never expressed regret. His love for Korea and its people only grew stronger over time.

My Grandfather Today

At 90 years old, my grandfather remains a figure of resilience and dedication. Although COVID-19 affected his health, he continues to be an active member of his community. Until recently, he served as the chair of the Colombian South-West Korean War Veteran Association, a role he took immense pride in. Through this position, he advocated for the welfare of veterans and worked tirelessly to raise awareness about Colombia's contributions to the Korean War.

His wife shares his commitment. As the former association's secretary, she has been a steadfast partner in his efforts to preserve the legacy of the Colombian soldiers. Together, they have ensured that the sacrifices of their generation are not forgotten.

One of my grandfather's greatest joys is sharing his memories with others. He loves meeting visitors, especially younger generations who are eager to learn about the war. Despite his age, his passion for telling these stories is unwavering. He often emphasizes the importance of remembering the past, not just to honor the fallen, but also to inspire future generations to strive for peace and cooperation.

My grandfather's life today is a testament to the enduring bonds forged during the Korean War. His dedication to his comrades, his family, and the legacy of his service is an inspiration to all who know him.

My Life in Korea

I am currently finalizing my studies in Global Cooperation at Sookmyung Women's University and I plan to remain in Korea for the time being. Living in Korea has been a transformative experience, both professionally and personally. As a student focusing on International Cooperation for Development, I have delved deeply into Korea's history and its modern success story.

Being an immigrant in Korea has also given me a unique perspective on global migration issues. I have seen firsthand the challenges and opportunities that migration brings, and I am committed to addressing these issues in my future work.

As a Korean War veteran descendant, I have had opportunities to participate in forums, seminars, and political meetings that have enriched my understanding of Korea's history and its global role. These experiences have also allowed me to advocate for stronger ties between Colombia and Korea and strengthen my ability to serve as a bridge between both nations.

Every day, I am reminded of my grandfather's sacrifices and the legacy he left behind. His story inspires me to contribute to the ongoing friendship between our nations and to use my experiences to build a better future for others.

Santiago Gaona and Stephanie Arguello Gaona. Building 63, Seoul, South Korea (September 2019)

Stephanie Arguello, Park Jin (former Minister of Foreign Affairs), Ilayda Asimgil. Seoul-South Korea (2024)

A Message to the Younger Generation

The Korean War is more than just history—it is a testament to courage, resilience, and unity in the face of adversity. To the younger generation, I urge you to honor this legacy by remembering the sacrifices of those who fought for freedom.

Let their stories inspire you to build a world rooted in peace, innovation, and mutual respect. Heroes like my grandfather remind us that even in the darkest times, humanity's strength and compassion can light the way forward.

Stephanie Arguello, Valentina Rojas. Gyeryong World Military Culture Expo (2022)

A Step Forward

In memory of Juan B. Rojas
Written by Valentina Rojas Martinez

Juan B. Rojas
Second Colombia Battalion Soldier

Valentina Rojas Martinez
Hankuk University of Foreign Studies

About Me

My name is Valentina Rojas Martínez, and I am a second-year master's student in Biological Chemistry at Hankuk University of Foreign Studies in South Korea. My personal connection to Korea stems not only from my grandfather, Juan B. Rojas, a Korean War veteran, but also from my deep admiration for how a country once ravaged by war has transformed into a stable economy and a leader in technological innovation.

My first impression of Korea was not filled with good memories. As a child, I noticed that my grandfather avoided any conversation related to Korea. I vividly remember a time when my cousin and I were watching a documentary about the Korean War, and as soon as my grandfather saw it, he stood up and walked away. At that time, we didn't know he had fought in the war, but our aunts later explained that he had participated in this international conflict. As the years passed, he slowly began to share more stories about his experiences during the war, and with that, my curiosity about this distant

Valentina Rojas Martinez, Gyeryong World Military Culture Expo(2022)

My grandfather, Juan B Rojas, and Valentina Rojas Martinez on my 25-birthday celebration (2021)

country began to grow.

During my undergraduate studies in Colombia, I became more exposed to Korean culture through dramas and K-pop, which deepened my interest in visiting Korea. That curiosity eventually turned into determination, and I began preparing to pursue a master's degree in Korea. As a descendant of a Korean War veteran, I was eligible for a special scholarship program and applied in 2021 to join the class of 2022. I'll never forget the moment I found out I'd been selected for the scholarship—the news came early on Christmas Eve, and it instantly became the best Christmas gift I've ever received.

Korea has offered me the opportunity to grow academically and personally, as I had to face unique challenges as an immigrant in a very different cultural environment. During my first year, I dedicated myself to learning the Korean language, adapting to an entirely new language and culture. After completing my Korean studies, I officially began my master's program.

Colombia's Dedication

Colombia was the only South American country to participate in this conflict under the name 'Batallón Colombia,' contributing one infantry battalion and one frigate, totaling 5,100 men, 213 casualties and 448 wounded. The first infantry battalion arrived at the port of Busan on June 16, 1951, after a 25-day journey covering a distance of 14,973 kilometers. The battalion's main duties consisted of patrol operations. Their most notable participation included fierce combat in the battles for Monte Calvo (Hill 180) and Old Baldy (Hill 266), both of which were fought primarily against Chinese troops.

During the administration of Laureano Gómez Castro, Colombia was undergoing a period of recovery after one of the most violent and bloody internal conflicts in its history, which had left the country's economy unstable. By participating in the Korean War, Colombia sought to strengthen its trade and diplomatic relations with the United States. Additionally, Colombia did not have a well-established army at that time, and its involvement in the war was instrumental in consolidating this institution.

While in Korea, Colombian soldiers mainly interacted with Spanish-speaking members of the U.S. Army, most of whom were Puerto Rican, as well as Ethiopian troops and a few South Korean soldiers.

The Colombian soldiers who participated in the conflict were between 16 and 22 years old. Most of them had never left the country, did not speak English, and had never experienced winter. Being a tropical country, Colombia had no equivalent to the harsh winters of the Korean Peninsula, making the extreme cold an additional challenge for the soldiers already facing brutality and cruelty of war.

At the end of the conflict, the brave Colombian soldiers returned home and were welcomed by their families and communities as heroes. They not only brought honor and pride to the country, showcasing to the world the courage, bravery, and determination of Colombians, but also left future generations one of the strongest bilateral relationships Colombia maintains in international politics: its alliance with South Korea. One of the phrases that best represents this bond is: "Brothers in war, brothers in peace."

The Colombian Battalion at the United Nations Memorial Cemetery in Busan, South Korea

My grandfather during Korean war, working as a barber (1952)

My Grandfather's Story

My grandfather was 22 years old when he participated in the Korean War. He joined the conflict in 1952 and took part in the Battle of Hill 180, also known as Monte Calvo, as well as Old Baldy (Hill 266). Since I was a child, I learned that asking him about Korea or his experience in the war was not easy because the scars that war leaves on a soul can be deep, and he preferred silence.

As the years went by, my grandfather started opening more and shared his experiences in Korea with us. He never spoke of the hardships or horrors he experienced, but preferred to speak about the good moments. He told us, for example, about the first time he saw snow: when he woke up, everything around him was covered in white and gray tones. He thought they had been attacked until one of his comrades explained that it was snow. He said it felt like a dream and always remembered that moment with one phrase: "Mija, it was really cold those days."

He also shared lessons about the importance of teamwork and trust in his comrades, which was essential to being able to rest at night in the middle of the war. Among his anecdotes, he also recalled his first experience with a type of food he never imagined trying.

My grandfather standing in front of a Colombian publication that paid tribute to him for his service during the Korean War (2020)

In memory of my grandfather (2023)

One day, when I finally got the courage to ask him why he had enlisted, his answer was simple yet striking: "Well, Mija, they told me I was going on a very long trip by ship and that I would get to see the ocean. I had never seen the ocean, so I enlisted." At that time, my grandfather was already serving his mandatory military service when he was offered the opportunity to join the Second Colombia Battalion, a unit that would support the UN in the war.

My grandfather was originally from the department of Tolima, a region in the interior of the country. In his time, traveling to the Colombian coast was not easy, so the possibility of seeing the ocean and boarding a ship fascinated him. You should have seen the smile on his face when he told us about his first impression of the sea, it was like watching a little child overwhelmed with pure joy. He also related his journey to Asia—his first time seeing Flying Fish, hearing the sounds of howler monkeys, and listening to the songs of unfamiliar birds as they crossed the Panama Canal.

Perhaps his reason for enlisting is not the most heroic answer one might expect, but the lesson he left to his children and grandchildren is invaluable: it is worth taking a leap into adventure without overthinking the outcomes. A small act of bravery can change history.

My grandfather never imagined that his courageous decision to enlist in a foreign war would contribute to the rebuilding of a nation that was, at the time, ravaged by conflict. South Korea rose from the hardship and devastation of war by believing in its people and investing in growth, eventually becoming a global leader in fields such as engineering, research, and entertainment, as well as one of the world's most stable economies. It is also a country that has generously shared its knowledge and development experience with my homeland, Colombia.

My grandfather passed away at the age of 92 in 2023. I always wished he could have come to Korea and seen with his own eyes the country he helped protect. I would have loved to show him how beautiful and incredible Korea is, how efficient its systems are, and how comfortable life is here. However, life did not allow me to have that precious moment with him, but even so, I know he has accompanied me every step of my journey here.

One of my greatest motivations to honor Colombia's name is to pay tribute to him and to the 5,100 brave Colombian soldiers who stood firm in their decision to embark on an international conflict.

Message to Future Generations

My message to future generations is not only to remember that "those who do not know their history are condemned to repeat it," but also to recognize that understanding our past empowers us to become a better version of those who came before us. I choose to believe that the future we are building holds more promise than we can currently imagine.

My grandfather drinking coffee in viewpoint of Ibague, Tolima, Colombia (2021)

My grandfather's 92nd birthday celebration (2021)

In light of that, I want to share the lesson my grandfather indirectly taught me through his participation in the war: it is worth stepping forward. Even if that first step seems difficult, take it with determination and certainty that life's plans are wiser than our own judgement.

When we take that step, we do not know what the future holds, but like my grandfather, taking it with courage can not only lead you on a journey that transforms your own story, but also the history of a country, influencing the lives of future generations. Live each moment as a gift, for though our time is short, the impact of our choices may ripple far beyond our years.

ETHIOPIA

Period of participation	1951.05.07 ~ 1965.01	
Total number of troop deployments	3,518	
Ground Troops	Infantry battalion	1
	Forces	1,271 men
Injuries of UN forces attended	KIA	122
	WIA	536
	Total	658

The monument of participation in the Korean War is located in Geunhwa-dong, Chuncheon-si, Gangwon-do

Echoes of Honor

The Legacy of Korean War Veterans and Their Descendants' Journey

In memory of Gemechu Guta

Written by Wakjira Gemechu

Gemechu Guta
Corporal

Wakjira Gemechu
Kunsan National University

About Me

Model photography for a t-shirt brand (2022)

My father and I when I was 4 years old A lifetime of love (1993)

I am Wakjira Gemechu, the youngest son of Veteran Gemechu Guta and I'm from Ethiopia. Since my father always talked about the Korean War and showed the pictures to our family, I have been both familiar and curious about Korea since I was young. The Korean folk song Arirang, Arirang, Arariyo, that my father taught me has been familiar since I was a child. I also remember watching Korea's soccer match in the 2002 World Cup during my teenage years and my family supported Korea while singing Oh Pilseung Korea, a team chant, which means Oh Victory to Korea. I especially have a vivid memory of my family cheering and celebrating when Korea won the match against Italy.

I first came to Korea in December 2012 through a scholarship program jointly run by KCCI [Korea Chamber of Commerce and Industry] and KOICA [Korea International

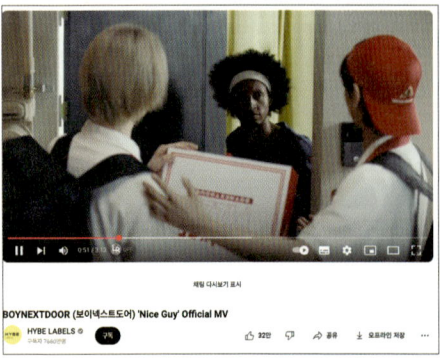

Featured as a background actor in a K-pop MV (2024)

Cooperation Agency]. I took Korean language classes and received technical training in the Department of Mechanical Engineering at Kunsan National University, later completing an advanced Korean language course at Soongsil University. Now, I work at a mechanical parts manufacturing company and occasionally appear in movies, K-pop idol music videos, and commercials, enjoying my time in Korea.

My Life in Korea

Contributing to cultural connection

My life in Korea is sociable and active. I have adapted well and continue to gain experience by participating in various activities with a sense of historical responsibility. I have volunteered at multiple exchange events fostering connections between Korea and Ethiopia.

From 2017 to 2018, I served as the leader of the Ethiopia-Korean War Veterans Family Association in Korea, facilitating cultural exchanges and collaborations with many Korean individuals and organizations. As a host of the radio program "Gobez Crew" on the immigrant broadcasting station MWTV, I have actively shared news, history, and cultural insights not only about Ethiopia but also about Korea.

Vision Camp (2024)

Guest appearance on MWTV's migrant radio show (2017)

Passing down the history and legacy of UN veterans

I have taken on the role of sharing the history and values of UN veterans, ensuring that their sacrifices and contributions are remembered and honored. I have also engaged with young Korean students by participating in a workshop on the history of UN forces, held for middle and high school students in Uijeongbu. Attending for the second time allowed me to reconnect with students who remembered me from previous sessions, fostering deeper conversations about history and remembrance.

As a representative of the descendants of war veterans, I participated in an SBS News about the ongoing 70-year bond between South Korea and the Kagnew Battalion soldiers, helping to raise awareness of their legacy.

In 2023, to commemorate the 70th anniversary of the Korean Armistice Agreement

Joining a UN Forces history workshop with Uijeongbu students (2024)

Sharing stories about Ethiopian culture and my life in Korea with Uijeongbu students (2024)

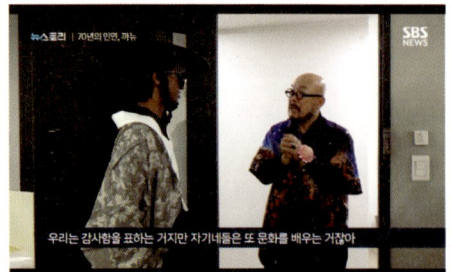
Talking with designer Lee Sang-bong before the UN uniform fashion show runway (2023)

Thumbnail from an interview with a descendant of a Korean War veteran (2022)

in 1953, I took part in the 'We Art! UNiform Runway' event in collaboration with the Uijeongbu Youth Foundation. This unique military fashion show, designed by world-renowned designer Lee Sang-bong, reinterpreted the uniforms of soldiers from the 16 UN countries that fought in the Korean War. As a descendant of a veteran, I walked the runway, not only enjoying the experience of being on stage, but also personally honoring the courage and sacrifice of my father's generation, who dedicated themselves to protecting South Korea's freedom.

Most recently, I visited the 28th Infantry Division and the DMZ, where my father was once stationed. During this two-day military experience program, I witnessed the dedication and strength of the South Korean military, reflecting on my father's service and on the enduring legacy of those who fought for Korea's freedom.

We Art! UNiform Runway (2023)

A visit to the DMZ and the 28th Infantry Division (2024)

Saving Korean citizens with the sacrifice and dedication I learned from my father

When the tragic accident occurred in Itaewon on Halloween in October 2022, I was present at the scene. In that urgent and critical moment, I instinctively attempted to resuscitate three unconscious individuals by performing CPR. It was an incredibly heartbreaking and shocking experience, but without hesitation, I focused on saving those who had collapsed.

I believe it was the sense of responsibility and courage I learned from my father that enabled me to act without fear. Following the incident, I received plaques of appreciation from the Consul of the Ethiopian Embassy, the Chief Monk of Cheonman Temple, and my company. I was also interviewed by Korean news outlets regarding the event.

With the Ethiopian consul and the head monk of Cheonman Temple (2023)

Interviewed by a news journalist about the Itaewon disaster (2023)

Plaque of appreciation for Itaewon disaster response from the Ethiopian Embassy and from my company (2023)

Ethiopia's Dedication in the Korean War

Deployment of the Kagnew Battalion

Kagnew was an elite unit of the Ethiopian Emperor's Guard, and the word Kagnew in Amharic means "victor" or "conqueror." Ethiopia was invaded by Italy in 1935 during World War II, but received no assistance from the international community. Drawing from this experience, Emperor Haile Selassie believed that even a small nation should uphold international justice. Between 1951 and 1954, he personally selected and ordered the deployment of a total of 3,518 troops, offering his personal blessing to the elite soldiers of the Emperor's Guard departing for Korea.

253 victories in 253 battles: the no-prisoners principle

The Kagnew Battalion upheld an unyielding military doctrine—the principle that not a single soldier would be captured by the enemy. This conviction drove them to fight to the very end, embodying the unit's indomitable spirit. They engaged in 253 battles, achieving victory in every single one, playing a crucial role in each conflict.

Even after the armistice, Ethiopia remained committed to Korea's recovery. The 4th and 5th Kagnew units were deployed to help rebuild the war-torn country. Ethiopian Red Cross nurses were sent to UN military hospitals, and Ethiopia continued to supply medical aid through the UNICEF [United Nations International Children's Emergency Fund] both during and after the war.

The Kagnew Battalion's withdrawal was carried out in phases, with the final troops departing in January 1965. Upon their return, Emperor Haile Selassie welcomed them as heroes, honoring their service with medals in recognition of their unwavering dedication and sacrifice.

My father upon arrival in Korea during the war (1951)

My father Gemechu Guta's combat medal

My father, Gemechu Guta went to Korea as part of the very first Ethiopian battalion consisting of 1185 troops. After he finished his mission, he went on to join the second Kagnew battalion and serve in the Korean War until his rotation in April 1953.

While the scout battalion was on duty, Gemechu Guta was working as the right-wing Corporal in the Battle of Mount Ley. When the enemy soldiers attacked and tried to surround the Ethiopian troops, the hero Gemechu threw a hand grenade and killed four of them in the middle.

Additionally, when soldiers Takele and Ayele were wounded and on the verge of being captured, Corporal Gemechu Guta bravely rescued them and transported them to a medical facility, ensuring their safety. In recognition of his valor and leadership, he was awarded a combat medal and a certificate of honor.

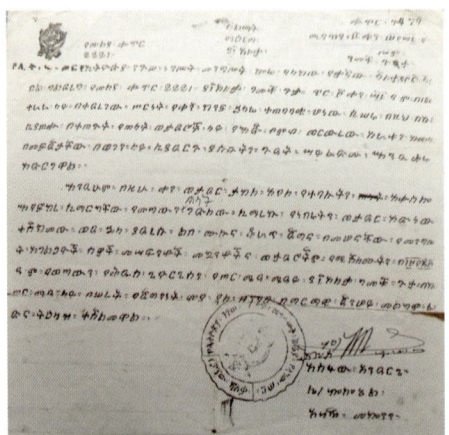

Certificate awarded to my father by the commander in Amharic (1954)

"This is to certify that soldier Gemechu Guta has served with distinction in the Kagnew Battalion during the Korean War, representing the Ethiopian Empire. He showed exemplary courage and commitment throughout the mission. His conduct has brought great honor not only to the battalion but also to his country. In recognition of his service, this certificate is issued by the order of the Commander.
May his bravery serve as an example for generations to come."

A portrait of my father taken during his service in the Korean War (1951)

Returning home from Korea after completing military service (1956)

My father's visit to Korea

My father had three sons, including me. After completing his military service, he worked as a lawyer at a private law firm. He was always proud to be one of the Ethiopian veterans of the Korean War. He often shared his experiences and stories. He taught me invaluable lessons about courage, responsibility, and confidence.

After the war, my father had the opportunity to visit Korea again. He was one of the fortunate few who witnessed firsthand how much the country had developed and transformed since the war. Deeply moved by Korea's remarkable progress, he strongly encouraged me to go there, learn as much as I could, and become a bridge between our two cultures and histories.

Now, as I live in Korea with a heart full of gratitude, I hold onto the greatest lesson my father ever taught me: confidence.

"Be confident in yourself. Believing in yourself is the first step to becoming a strong person."

My father after retiring from the military, beginning his new path as a lawyer (1960s)

A hero's certificate and medals awarded by Emperor Haile Selassie (1954)

A Message for the Future of Our Relationship

I hope that the alliance between Korea and Ethiopia will not remain just as a historical event, but continue to hold meaningful value for both the present and the future. We should re-examine the significance of the sacrifices and solidarity shown during the war, and bring them into a modern context.

Through social media, documentaries, and YouTube content, we can actively share our friendship, fostering positive awareness so that future generations naturally recognize this bond through commemorative projects and history education. This is crucial because a strong relationship is built through diplomacy at the government level as well as understanding sentiments of the people. By keeping these stories alive, we empower future generations to carry forward a legacy of mutual respect, gratitude, and lasting solidarity.

I am committed to playing my part in strengthening this connection and ensuring that our shared history continues to inspire and unite us.

My father revisiting Korea after more than 50 years (2007)

Echoes of Sacrifice

An Ethiopian Soldier's Journey and the Future We Must Build

In memory of Kebede Abate Wende

Written by Bethelehem Solomon Shenkute

Kebede Abate Wende
Private in the Second Kagnew Battalion

Bethelehem Solomon Shenkute
Hankuk University of Foreign Studies

About Me

Bethelehem Solomon Shenkute in Korea, traveling around the country (2023)

My name is Bethelehem Solomon Shenkute, Ha Eun-Byul 하은별 in Korean. I was born and raised in Addis Ababa, Ethiopia, a country with a rich history and strong values of resilience, justice, and community. Today, I live in Incheon, South Korea. I have completed my master's degree in International Studies in Hankuk University of Foreign Studies.

As a foreigner in Korea, I am often asked where I'm from. When I say Ethiopia, the reactions vary. The older generation expresses gratitude, recognizing Ethiopia's contributions during the Korean War and thanking me for my country's sacrifice. The younger generation, on the other hand, responds with, "Ah, the country of coffee!" Both reactions reflect different aspects of Ethiopia's identity: its historical ties with the Korean War and its global reputation as the birthplace of coffee. While I appreciate both, I hope that more young people will come to learn about the deep and meaningful friendship between our two nations beyond just coffee.

I came to Korea in 2021 to pursue my graduate studies. However, my journey to Korea was driven by more than academic goals. It was about following in the life-changing footsteps of my grandfather.

My grandfather on my mother's side, Kebede Abate Wende, was one of the brave Ethiopian soldiers who fought in the Korean War. His experiences shaped his life, his family, and even me, his grandchild. But I rarely knew about this part of my family's history.

My interest in Korea began through something entirely different: Korean television. I still remember the first time I was exposed to K-dramas. It was one fateful night in 10th grade of high school. My younger sister and I were baking, waiting for our bread to finish. I suggested we check out KBS World, a channel I had heard quite repetitively, might I add, from a classmate. That night, a weekend drama titled 사랑을 믿어요 (Believe in Love) was airing. That was the moment everything started.

From that time on, my sister and I became hooked on Korean dramas and entertainment shows. We spent weekends watching Korean dramas and TV shows such as Gag Concert and 2 Days & 1 Night, fascinated by the humor, culture, and storytelling. At the time, we didn't know much about Korea other than the brief history we learned during school history classes, but we loved what we saw on screen.

Then, one day, something unexpected happened. My grandmother visited us and saw us watching a Korean program. Curious, she asked what we were watching. When we told her, she smiled and said something that would change my life forever:

"Did you know your grandfather went to Korea?"

That was the first time I ever heard about his journey in Korea. That night, my grandmother told us about my grandfather's journey, how he had fought in the Korean War as part of the Kagnew Battalion, how the war had changed his life, and how he had later become a judge in Ethiopia.

Betheleehem at the Korean War Veterans' Memorial located in Addis Ababa, Ethiopia (2018)

Translation Volunteer work during the Ethiopian veterans' visit to Korea (2021)

Hearing his story sparked something inside me. I became obsessed with Korean history and culture. I started reading books, watching documentaries, and even learning the Korean language on my own. But I didn't stop there: I wanted to connect with my grandfather's legacy in a deeper, more meaningful way.

I began volunteering at the Ethiopian Korean War Veterans Association, where I worked with Korean visitors and honored Ethiopian veterans. During this time, I met Dr. Ha Ok-sun, a woman who would play a pivotal role in shaping my path to Korea. She became a mentor, guiding me in my studies and community work.

Thanks to her support, I was able to build a reputation in the field of Korea-Ethiopia relations. This ultimately led me to receive a recommendation from the Embassy of the Republic of Korea in Ethiopia, which opened the door for me to pursue my master's degree in Korea.

Now, as I walk through the streets of Korea, a nation that has become a global economic powerhouse, I think of my grandfather. I reflect on the war that shaped his life, the sacrifices he made, and how his grandchild would return to this land decades later—not as a soldier, but as a student continuing his legacy.

This is why I want to tell his story. Not just for him, but for all of us who believe in history, legacy, and the power of remembering.

Ethiopia During the Korean War: A Nation that Knew the Pain of Invasion

Many people are unaware that Ethiopia was one of the nations that sent troops to fight in the Korean War. When North Korea invaded South Korea in 1950, much of the world only watched as the nation faced destruction. Ethiopia, under the leadership of Emperor Haile Selassie, responded by sending elite soldiers to fight alongside the United Nations forces.

However, Ethiopia's decision to help Korea was not just about global diplomacy. It was deeply personal.

Less than two decades before the Korean War, Ethiopia itself had suffered a brutal invasion by Italian colonial forces. In 1935, Fascist Italy, under Benito Mussolini, invaded Ethiopia, forcing Emperor Haile Selassie into exile and subjecting the country to years of suffering. Although Ethiopia was eventually liberated in 1941, the trauma of foreign occupation was still fresh. Ethiopians understood what it meant to have their sovereignty threatened, to see their homes destroyed, and to fight against overwhelming odds for freedom.

This painful history shaped Ethiopia's unwavering commitment to South Korea's cause. Haile Selassie saw Korea's struggle as a reflection of Ethiopia's own past and believed it was his duty to stand on the side of justice.

Ethiopia's contribution came in the form of the Kagnew Battalions, an elite unit trained to the highest military standards. These soldiers were known for their courage, discipline, and unwavering loyalty. Unlike many other UN forces, the Ethiopian troops had a reputation for never surrendering on the battlefield. Their motto, instilled by the emperor, their commander-in-chief, was simple but powerful:

"Victory or Death."

Emperor Haile Selassie I (1970)
© wikimedia.org

Ethiopian soldiers in Korea © wikimedia.org

For Korea, the Ethiopian soldiers became symbols of international solidarity. They were exemplary soldiers, gaining victory in all the 253 battles they engaged in, with no war prisoners taken by the Chinese or North Korean soldiers. For Ethiopia, the war was a demonstration of its commitment to peace, justice, and global cooperation. For the individual soldiers who left their families behind, it was a life-changing experience—one that would shape their futures in ways they never imagined.

The Betrayal of Ethiopia's Heroes

At the time of the Korean War, Ethiopia was one of the most stable and economically promising nations in Africa. Our country was a leader in diplomacy, a founding member of the United Nations, and a model for modernization and development in the region. The country's participation in the Korean War was seen as an act of international responsibility, aligning Ethiopia with the values of freedom and sovereignty.

But history took a tragic turn.

In 1974, Emperor Haile Selassie's government was overthrown by a military junta known as the Derg, led by Mengistu Haile Mariam. This regime plunged Ethiopia into 17 years of dictatorship, repression, and bloodshed.

The new government aligned itself with the Soviet Union and North Korea, shifting

Ethiopian Soldiers during the Korean War (1953)
© U.S. Army Public Domain

Mengistu Haile Mariam - Leader of the dictatorship Derg regime (1977) © wikimedia.org

Ethiopia's foreign policy towards the communist bloc. As a result, the very soldiers who had once fought for Korea's freedom became political targets.

Many of the Kagnew Battalion veterans were accused of being traitors, and labeled as pro-Western sympathizers simply because they had fought alongside the United Nations. Some were arrested, tortured, or even executed under suspicion of supporting imperialist and capitalist ideologies. Others were silenced and forced into hiding, stripped of the honor they had earned on the battlefield.

Ethiopia, which had once stood as a beacon of stability and progress, collapsed into economic ruin, political oppression, and civil conflict. The heroes who had once been celebrated for defending freedom in Korea were now being punished by their own homeland.

It is a bitter irony that while Korea prospered and remembered the sacrifices of Ethiopian soldiers with deep gratitude, those same veterans faced hardship and neglect back home. The country they had fought for flourished, while their own country fell into darkness and despair.

For decades, their sacrifices were forgotten by Ethiopia's rulers. It was only years later, after the fall of the dictatorship, that Ethiopia's role in the Korean War was acknowledged once again, and the remaining Kagnew Battalion veterans were finally honored for their service.

Korea and Ethiopia Today: A Friendship that Endures

The story of Ethiopia's involvement in the Korean War is more than just a historical event. It is a lesson in resilience, sacrifice, and justice. Ethiopia knew the pain of invasion and it fought for Korea out of a shared understanding of what it meant to lose freedom. The Kagnew Battalion fought not just for Korea, but for the values of sovereignty, dignity, and justice that Ethiopia itself had struggled to protect.

Decades after the Korean War, Korea has never forgotten Ethiopia's sacrifice. Ethiopian veterans are still honored in Korea, with annual commemorations and special programs inviting them to witness the country they once fought to protect. The deep gratitude of the Korean people remains evident, as Ethiopia is recognized as a brother nation that stood by Korea during its darkest time.

This historical bond has evolved into strong diplomatic and economic cooperation. Korea actively supports Ethiopia's development through organizations like KOICA, funding projects in healthcare, education, agriculture, and technology. Korean businesses, including Hyundai, Samsung, and LG, have expanded into Ethiopia, contributing to industrial growth and job creation. Even individuals who deeply respect Ethiopians for their contributions give what they can to help Ethiopia develop.

Through continued government partnerships, trade agreements, and humanitarian efforts, Korea is giving back to Ethiopia, ensuring that its shared history of sacrifice becomes a foundation for mutual growth and long-term friendship. The relationship is no longer just about the past, but about building a future together.

The Story of Priv. Kebede Abate Wende

My grandfather's life was a testament to courage, sacrifice, and unwavering dedication to justice. As an eighteen-year-old, he enlisted in the palace guards for Emperor Haile Selassie, a decision that would shape the course of his life. Soon after, he found himself on a journey far from home, answering the call to serve in the Korean War. He came to Korea as a driver in the second Kagnew Battalion, part of Ethiopia's noble contribution to the war effort.

During his year of service, he witnessed firsthand the devastation that war left in its wake. The destruction of entire communities, the plight of children left orphaned, and the sorrow of parents forced to send their children to the battlefield deeply moved him. The experience changed him, instilling in him an even greater sense of duty—not only to his country but to humanity as a whole.

Upon returning to Ethiopia, he set his sights on a new mission: to build a better future through justice. He enrolled in law school and became a judge, earning a reputation as a fair and compassionate figure in his community. His dedication to helping others extended beyond the courtroom. He engaged in volunteer work and was known for his kindness, inspiring those around him with his selfless service. He was deeply admired and respected in his community—not only for his role as a judge, but also for the wisdom and strength he shared as a mentor.

His commitment to justice and his esteemed reputation played a crucial role in his survival when the imperial government was overthrown by a dictatorial regime. While many were persecuted during the transition, his recognized contributions to society served as his shield, allowing him to continue his life's work.

To my mother, he was more than a public servant; he was a loving and family-oriented man. She recalls the values he instilled in her, constantly reminding her to be

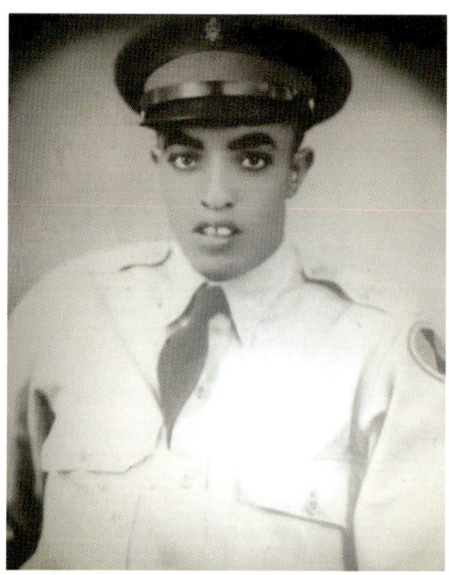

My grandfather Priv. Kebede Abate Wende soon after he enlisted in the palace guard (1949)

My grandfather with my mother (1972)

kind to everyone, regardless of their circumstances. Sadly, he passed away when she was in middle school, leaving behind a legacy that continues to inspire our family.

My grandfather's journey, from a young soldier fighting for freedom in a foreign land to a judge committed to justice and community service, embodies resilience and hope. His story is not just a chapter in our family's history, but also a reminder of the power of service, sacrifice, and unwavering dedication to making the world a better place.

A Message to the Younger Generation: Learning from History

To young people in Korea, I urge you to remember your history. The peace and prosperity you enjoy today exist because of the sacrifices made by people from all over the world, including my grandfather. Your grandparents and great-grandparents endured war and hardship so that future generations could live in freedom. History warns us that peace is fragile; it must be protected, nurtured, and never taken for granted.

To young people around the world, I want you to understand the cost of forgetting history. Today, we see the devastating impact of wars, refugee crises, socio-economic and political instability, and widening inequalities. Conflicts continue to tear nations apart, and people suffer because lessons from the past are ignored. The philosopher George Santayana once said, "Those who cannot remember the past are condemned to repeat it." My grandfather fought in a war that was not his own, believing in a cause greater than himself. His story is proof that we are all connected and that the suffering of one nation can ripple across the world. If we fail to learn from history, we risk repeating the same mistakes that have caused so much pain before.

The choices we make today will define the world of tomorrow. Will we allow division, hatred, and violence to shape our future, or will we choose unity, justice, and peace? We must never allow such forces to define our world or silence the lessons of those who came before us.

If my grandfather, a mere 18-year-old Ethiopian soldier, could travel across the world to fight for people he had never met and return home to build a life of service, then we, too, have the power to make a difference. This is not just his story; it is our story, a testament to courage, sacrifice, and the enduring strength of the human spirit. Let us honor that legacy by becoming the generation that remembers, unites, and builds a better world—for all of us.

FRANCE

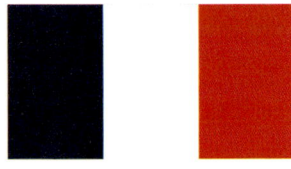

Period of participation	1950.07.22 ~ 1965.06	
Total number of troop deployments	3,421	
Ground Troops	Infantry battalion Forces	1 1,185 men
Navy	Destroyer	1
Injuries of UN forces attended	KIA WIA MIA POW Total	262 1,008 7 12 1,289

The monument of participation in the Korean War is located in Pajang-dong, Jangan-gu, Suwon-si, Gyeonggi-do

Silent Hero:

My Grandfather, a French Veteran in the Korean War

In memory of Bernard Prigl d'Ondel
Written by Alice Prigl d'Ondel

Bernard Prigl d'Ondel
French Battalion Soldier

Alice Prigl d'Ondel
Hankuk University of Foreign Studies

About Me

Alice Prigl d'Ondel

My name is Alice Prigl d'Ondel, I'm from France and I've been living in Korea for over four years now. When I consider carefully, I realize that my relationship with Korea may have been a result of fate. Indeed, growing up in the 2000s, I recall watching Korean dramas with my sister at a time when K-dramas and K-culture were not as widely popular as they are today, especially in France. Never having traveled abroad, I had no real knowledge of Korea, but I found myself captivated by the stories, the culture, and the uniqueness of a country that seemed so far from me.

And then, one day in October 2020, my aunt contacted me to let me know about a letter from the Korean embassy in France that revealed something unexpected that immediately deepened my connection to Korea: my grandfather, Bernard Prigl d'Ondel, had served as a Korean War Veteran, making me eligible to apply for the Scholarship Program for Descendants of UN Korean War Veterans and study in Korea. This revelation completely changed my life. I applied and got the news around Christmas that I was accepted. I moved to Korea in February 2021 to study at Hankuk University of Foreign Studies. Suddenly, Korea was not only a country I had admired as a little child, but also a country that shared a deeper history and legacy that connected me to my family.

Now, as a student finishing my studies in International Studies this summer, I have had the chance over the past four years to dive deeper into the history and culture, while also observing firsthand the "한강의 기적" (Miracle of the Han River), a unique example of rapid economic growth. Studying in this environment has been inspiring, and I plan to pursue a career in development to help apply this model in other parts of the world.

France's Dedication

France's involvement in the Korean War is often overlooked, even within its own national history and the school curriculum, despite being a testament to respecting international law and its contribution to global peace efforts during the early stages of the Cold War. On July 22, 1950, following the British, Turkish, and Australian contingents, France declared its participation in a multinational force aimed at restoring the territorial integrity of South Korea after the North Korean invasion.

Despite still being in the wake of the devastation of World War II and still recovering from its own challenges, France established a volunteer battalion composed of active military personnel and the reserves under the leadership of General Monclar, a hero of both World Wars. This battalion became an emblem of courage and resilience, enduring extreme conditions and limited resources, yet still participating in some of the most significant battles of the war.

The volunteers of the French Battalion of the UN in Korea conducting a flamethrower test
"Le Bataillon français de l'ONU en Corée" by Gabriel Appay, © 1952

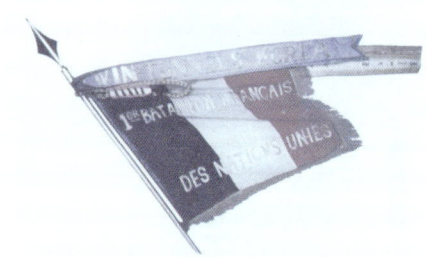

Flag of the French Battalion in Korea
Pierre Ferrari, © 1996

The French graves in the UN Cemetery of Tanggok, Busan
© unmck.or.kr

One of the most remarkable episodes was during the Battle of Wonju in January 1951, where the French Battalion, alongside other allied forces, played an essential role in halting the Chinese advance. Their decisive bayonet charge gained international recognition. Their continued involvement in battles like the Battle of Twins Tunnels and the Battle of Chipyong-ni, where they withstood assaults from four Chinese divisions for three days, contributed to a successful counteroffensive by the 8th Army. This solidified their reputation and earned them multiple American Presidential citations, including a third one after their courageous stand in Hwachon in the spring of 1951.

As the war continued, from the bloody Battle of Heartbreak Ridge to the fierce resistance at Chongwon where they repelled a Chinese offensive, and through the winter and spring battles of 1953 that prevented North Korean and Chinese forces from advancing towards Seoul, the battalion proved its valor time and time again.

By the time of the armistice in June 1953, France had lost 262 soldiers, including 9 officers and 26 non-commissioned officers, with many of them laid to rest in the international cemetery in Busan. 3,421 French soldiers had served in Korea, leaving a lasting legacy and affirming France's role in Korea's history.

My grandfather, Bernard Prigl d'Ondel (2017)

My Grandfather's Story

My grandfather, Bernard Prigl d'Ondel, was born on December 21, 1924, in Beirut, Lebanon. Driven by his values, he joined the French resistance forces during World War II and was demobilized in late 1945. After four years as a civilian working in a paint factory where the fumes made him sick every day, he turned on the radio as usual, and one day heard a call for soldiers to join the war in Korea. At that time, my grandfather had no idea what or where Korea was, but he felt compelled to respond and volunteered to join the first French contingent that arrived in December 1950.

Upon arriving in Korea, he was first struck by the realities of poverty. The country was far poorer than he had ever imagined on the long way to get there. He was also shocked by the weather. It was cold, far colder than he had ever prepared for, and none of the soldiers were truly ready for such conditions. The terrain was unforgiving, and the battles were relentless. Like so many wartime tragedies, his most sorrowful memory was carrying a wounded comrade on his back through the chaos of mines and bombings, only to realize upon arrival that his friend had not survived. The weight of that moment stayed with him for the rest of his life. In January, to his dismay, he was reassigned to Japan, where, thanks to his linguistic skills in French, English, and Arabic, he was

Some pictures my grandfather took during his service in Korea

responsible for coordinating the transport of wounded soldiers to American hospitals. It was during this period that he purchased a camera and began documenting the war through photography.

In April 1951, he finally rejoined the battalion in Korea, where he fought in treacherous mountainous battles, including at Heartbreak Ridge. Even amidst the chaos, he continued capturing the reality of war, taking more than 400 photographs that now serve as a vital and precious record of the French soldiers' experience in Korea.

After a year of service, his mission was complete and he returned to France, quickly establishing a career in electronics. In 1958, my grandfather married and had three children, living a quiet life in the Paris region. Despite his remarkable journey, he never opened up about his time in Korea with our family, not even my father, until I applied for this Scholarship Program. Through the scholarship, I got the chance to grow closer to my grandfather, learn more about him, and connect with him in a way I hadn't before, especially since he had always been so reserved. October 2020 marked the beginning of a cherished time when we began to uncover and appreciate the full depth of his legacy. He recently passed away, exactly one month before his 100th birthday, leaving behind a legacy of courage, sacrifice, and an invaluable visual testimony of

A picture my grandfather took of his brothers-in-arms on the boat to Korea (1950)

"On the boat taking them to Korea, the French expected a short war."
- Lieutenant-Colonel Cadeau, military historian at the French Defense Historical Service (SHD) and author of La guerre de Corée

history. At his funeral, he was posthumously awarded the Legion of Honour, France's highest distinction, for his service during World War II and in the Korean War, a fitting tribute to his exceptional service and the legacy he left in history.

He often told me, especially before his passing, how much he wished he could have returned to Korea to witness the incredible changes it had undergone. He was always deeply impressed by the resilience of the Korean people and the remarkable transformation of the country. This was something he spoke about with great admiration, reflecting on the strength and determination of Korea to rebuild and thrive after the war.

A Message to the Future Relationship

As I reflect on my grandfather's incredible journey in Korea, I am reminded of how important the present moment is for the youth and how fortunate we are to live in peace. Indeed, at 27 years old, Korea I see today is a not only a modern, peaceful, and thriving country, but also a far cry from the devastated land my grandfather encountered at the exact same age. While he arrived in a country torn by war and poverty, I live in Korea that is now built on resilience, strength, and transformation. Considering how far Korea has come, we must carry forward the legacies of those who fought for peace and survival. My grandfather's story serves as a powerful reminder that history is not just a collection of dates and facts, but a long-lived reality shaped by real people who made profound sacrifices.

We inherit a world full of vast possibilities and great challenges, whether it is advancing technologies, addressing climate change, or striving for peace in a divided world. But to create meaningful change, we need to learn from the past and remember the legacies of those who came before us and are slowly leaving us.

USA / REPUBLIC OF KOREA

8240th Army Unit	Date of Establishment June 1, 1949 Date of Disbandment July 27, 1953 (Absorbed into the Republic of Korea Army after the Korean War Armistice)
Primary Functions	- Defense of islands and coastal waters in the West Sea - Collection of military intelligence on North Korea - Infiltration and guerrilla warfare operations against North Korea - Execution of sabotage missions
Affiliations	- United States Far East Command (FECOM) - United Nations Partisan Infantry Korea (UNPIK) - Republic of Korea Army (ROKA)

A Forgotten Fighter
from a Forgotten Unit in a Forgotten War

In memory of Kyung Jin Choi

Written by Monika Choi Stoy

Kyungjin Choi
Commander

Monika Choi Stoy
U.S. Army Captain

About me

C. Monika Stoy at Mount Vernon, VA for George Washington's 293rd birthday celebration (February 2025)

I am C. Monika Stoy, the daughter of Choi, Kyung Jin and Ji, Haesook. My family immigrated to the United States in 1973, and I joined the U.S. Army in 1975. I retired from the U.S. Army as a Captain after having served for twenty years. I have a Master's degree in Adult Education from North Carolina State University. While in the Army, I served with airborne units and earned the U.S., German, French, Italian, and Germany airborne wings. I served in Operation Provide Comfort in Northern Iraq in 1991.

I am now a military historian as well as the president of Outpost International, Society of the 3rd Infantry Division, a non-profit veterans' organization dedicated to the memory of the 3rd Infantry Division, U.S. Army and its veterans. This outpost organizes historical seminars on World War II and the Korean War both in the United States and overseas, and participates in commemorations in France, Germany, Austria, and Korea.

In recognition of my work in France, I was awarded the French Legion of Honor in 2023 and named an honorary citizen of several cities, including Mont St Michel, Montélimar, and Saint Tropez, where I also received the Gold Medal in 2024. As the daughter of Choi Kyung Jin, a partisan commander in the 8240 Army Unit, I give presentations on the unit and its American advisors to raise awareness of their role in the Korean War. I serve as the U.S. representative for the 8240 Army Unit Veterans' Association and was honored with the Republic of Korea Prime Minister's Medal in 2015 for my contributions to Korean War remembrance efforts.

To honor my father and his fellow partisans, my husband and I made several donations in his name. His name is now on the Circles of Distinction wall at the NMUSA [National Museum of the United States Army]. We also funded a tribute to the 8240 Army Unit, including a memorial tree, a commemorative brick at NMUSA, and a unit stone at the Airborne and Special Operations Museum in Fayetteville, North Carolina.

As an American, I am grateful for the United States' role in the Korean War as it fought to reunite Korea after northern Korea attacked in June 1950. I deeply appreciate the sacrifices of the many American service members who died in Korea, though I regret that the country remains divided despite their efforts. I also emphasize to those I speak with, that the Korean War was a Korean civil war and that the greatest sacrifices were made by the hundreds of thousands of Korean soldiers who fought and died for their country, along with the countless civilians. Having been born and raised in Korea, I am saddened by all that was lost by innocent Koreans and am bitter over the continued division of the country, the result of a misguided decision to divide the country in 1945 that ignored the Korean people's will for unity and independence.

8240 AU Unit Stone at the Airborne and Special Operations Museum in Fayetteville, NC

8240 AU Memorial at ROK Special Warfare Command HQ

My Father's Story

My father, Choi, Kyungjin, was born in Pyongyang on March 9, 1928 as the fourth of seven children in a wealthy family. He attended Kyungshin Middle School, a Christian Mission School founded in 1885 by the famous missionary Horace G. Underwood. It was the first Christian missionary school in Korea. He went on to attend both middle school and high school at Kyungshin. He was unable to visit his own family in Pyongyang due to the division of the country after the Japanese surrender in August 1945. Sadly, he never saw his family again after that time. Until his dying day, it was his wish to see Korea reunited and to find out what had happened to his family. He also retained a burning hatred of the communists who had destroyed his life.

He graduated from Kyungshin High School in June 1949. Upon the recommendation of his principal, he applied and got accepted to Sung Kyun Kwan University and began his studies in the summer of that year. A tragic postscript to this story is that his Kyungshin High School classmates who entered the military academy were all killed in action as cadets during the early stages of the Korean War in 1950.

During his time at university, he served as freshman class president. While there, his Kyungshin High School principal recommended he join an organization being recruited

Choi, Kyungjin as University Class President (1949)

Choi, Kyungjin in 1951

Haeju Landing Operation
20 OCT

by the U.S. Army's KMAG [Korean Military Advisory Group]. This organization was named the KLO [Korean Liaison Organization], and its purpose was to gather intelligence on military and political activities in northern Korea. The Americans were looking for northern Koreans who could blend in with the general population, as the communist system in northern Korea possessed a highly developed security apparatus. Strangers were always under suspicion and challenged– a KLO agent had to be able to think fast on his feet and not become flustered. My father spoke the distinctive northern Korean dialect, knew the geography of northern Korea especially Pyongyang and its surrounding area, and he was vehemently anti-communist.

He conducted numerous missions behind the enemy lines, even reaching the Yalu River in October 1950 to watch the Chinese forces cross into North Korea. He described seeing them "thick as ants" as they crossed the river into northern Korea. Trying to return to friendly lines from this mission, my father and his team were "captured" by soldiers of what was likely the 1st Cavalry Division, the furthest most-north UN unit in western Korea in October 1950 and the first unit to be attacked by Chinese forces. My father remembers the distinctive 1st Cavalry Division's yellow and black patch featuring a horse's head. He identified himself and his team as members of KLO, providing a pass code for them to verify with KMAG. During their four-day detention, they were treated humanely in accordance with the rules of war—provided with food and not subjected to mistreatment—before being released to KLO control.

I have a photograph of my father labeled "Haeju Landing Operation 20 OCT," referring to a mission in October 1950 that was part of a series of KLO landings carried out approximately one week after Pyongyang fell to UN forces. Although I have not yet located official documentation of this specific operation, the date coincides with the American 187th Airborne Regimental Combat Team's assault at Sukchon and Sunchon. It is likely that the Haeju landing was part of a broader effort to capture or block the escape of Kim Il Sung and members of his government as they fled Pyongyang.

Choi, Kyung Jin with fellow partisans on Jiri Mountain in early 1951

Choi, Kyungjin with fellow 8240 AU unit leaders in summer 1951

Choi, Kyungjin with fellow partisans on Christmas of 1952 or 1953

In January 1951, during an intelligence mission in his hometown of Pyongyang—which he had not seen since Korea's division in 1945—my father unexpectedly spotted his eldest brother, a former city hall official. When he called out, his brother recognized him and warned that the family had told the communists occupying their home that he had been killed by South Korean forces, and that being identified would put him in grave danger. They arranged to meet with their father the next morning, but overnight, my father's unit received orders to withdraw. He was never able to see his father, and this encounter would be the last time he had any contact with his family. Days later, on January 4, 1951, Chinese forces recaptured Seoul.

Another dangerous mission my father told me about was his activities in counter-guerilla operations on Jiri Mountain. Large numbers of northern Korean regular army soldiers had been cut off in southern Korea in September 1950, after the landings at Incheon and the breakout from the Pusan Perimeter. Many of these soldiers gathered on Jiri Mountain in Jeolla Province of southwest Korea. This area had been the hideout for bandits and rebels for hundreds of years due to its rugged terrain and sparse population. These soldiers had been reorganized by their officers and were conducting raids against the United Nations forces supply lines and rear area facilities with some success. Although my father never provided me with specific details of what his element did and exactly who they worked for, he had a picture of his four-man team on one of the peaks of Jiri Mountain and told me that they had been apprehended by ROK forces while they were on their mission. They were all badly beaten and one member of his team died from his ill-treatment, but they were eventually released to the U.S. control after their status as partisans was confirmed.

In July 1951, KLO became a part of the 8240th Army Unit United Nations Korean Partisans, Korea. These brave men and women undertook guerrilla operations behind enemy lines, such as attacks against fixed targets such as bridges, tunnels, and other important facilities or intelligence gathering missions. Most of these 10,000 to 15,000 partisans had escaped from northern Korea to islands off the western coast after the Chinese entered the war and forced UN forces to retreat from the north in late 1950. Vehemently anti-communist, these people resisted the reimposition of the communist system in their towns and villages, but were simply no match for the communists.

The U.S. Army had learned of their existence and saw an opportunity to support these anti-communist fighters, using them in enemy rear areas to tie down enemy forces. The unit was given training, weapons, uniforms, and other necessary equipment by the U.S. Army, and American advisers assigned them their missions. They were inserted either by sea, where the Allied navy had complete control of the waters, or by land infiltration. Land infiltration was extremely dangerous, as they had to wear either enemy uniforms or civilian clothes for the operation. While departing from friendly lines could be properly coordinated, re-entering was perilous, as trigger-happy soldiers, upon seeing personnel in enemy uniforms or civilian clothes moving along the demarcation line in no-man's land, were more likely to shoot first and ask questions later. My father served in two units, Donkey 6 and Wolfpack. He was never paid but would receive rice or occasionally some extra blankets. He was provided with his uniform with all the necessary combat equipment needed for his missions, and he lived in a military camp when not on a mission.

In June 1953, the Korean partisans of 8240 Army Unit, until then with no official status in the Republic of Korea, were integrated into the ROK Army as 8250 Army Unit. They continued their activities, still under U.S. direction, until June 1954, when the unit was disbanded and the partisans were offered positions in the ROK military. My father, who was a mid-level partisan unit commander at the approximate grade of Captain, was offered entry into the ROK Army as a 2nd Lieutenant. He declined. He was insulted at being offered such a low rank. He also believed he would never be fully trusted by South Korean soldiers because of his northern Korean dialect and his service as a partisan, and he didn't want to serve in an army where he was not trusted. He was a survivor and was determined to make his own way, starting from scratch in rebuilding ROK. He hadn't been paid by either the U.S. Army or the Republic of Korea; he received rations from the U.S. Army, that was all.

Choi, Kyungjin with American advisor and other partisans on airfield sometime in 1952~1953

Choi, Kyungjin with American pilots sometime in 1952~1953

My Father after the Korean War

After the war, my parents remained in Seoul and our family grew to include five children. My parents saved money and bought a hanok, a traditional Korean house, in Gahaedong not far from the Blue House, the executive office of the president of ROK. My parents owned a profitable sesame oil business. My two older brothers attended Kyung Shin High School, my father's old school. I attended elementary and middle school in Seoul, and emigrated with my family in 1973, during my first year of high school.

My family settled in Northern Virginia and my parents worked hard to establish a new life in the United States. My father never spoke to me about his Korean War service with the partisans until I served with a U.S. Special Operations unit in the early 1990s. It was only then that I learned he had been a partisan, and even then, he was reluctant to speak about his experiences. I had to draw his story from him a piece at a time, and there are many things I wish I had asked him then, but after a few minutes he would just say "tomorrow" and continue on with his day.

He did share with me pictures he had kept from his service with the KLO and the 8240 Army Unit. He is one of the very few who have photos from that period, and the Korean historians I correspond with are amazed to see them, as such images are quite rare.

Choi, Kyungjin at the Korean War Veterans Memorial in Washington, DC in 1998

My father gained American citizenship and he was very proud to be an American, while at the same time he remained proud of his Korean heritage. He was always complimentary of the American soldiers with whom he had served in the Korean War. He believed the U.S. – ROK alliance was indispensable to the security of both countries. He had made the decision to immigrate to the United States in 1973 because he wanted greater opportunities for his children to attend good schools and establish good careers in a free society. The ROK of the early 1970s had not yet experienced the economic miracle which would later raise it to one of the top ten economies in the world. He was concerned over the unstable political situation in the ROK and the continued tensions between North and South Korea. I am deeply grateful to my parents for the sacrifices they made for me and my siblings. We had a well-established life in Korea, but my father envisioned an even better future for us in the U.S. My father passed away on February 3, 2009. I think of him every day with the deepest gratitude for the sacrifices he made for me and my family.

A Message for Today

I believe the U.S.–ROK political and military alliance remains critical for both countries. As the U.S.'s security and economic interests in Asia gain ever greater importance, the ROK's role as an ally and friend continues to grow, with the ROK being an indispensable partner in maintaining peace and stability in Asia.

I am concerned that the younger generation, both in the U.S. and in the ROK, have forgotten the lessons of the Korean War, and that younger Koreans especially lack appreciation for the post-war sacrifices and achievements of their grandparents and parents in building today's Republic of Korea. Younger Koreans also fail to understand THE KOREAN WAR IS NOT OVER!

The 27 July 1953 armistice was not signed by the Republic of Korea and a state of war still exists between North and South Korea. Despite the past 72 years of relative calm, this reality calls for great vigilance and preparedness by every South Korean citizen.

WE REMEMBER

By: M. Garvey

Those we left there in the cold
We remember, we remember
Have no fears of growing old
Oh do we remember

Those who fell in prison yards
We remember, we remember
Savage weather savage guards
Oh do we remember

Those who died face down in mud
We remember, we remember
Asian soil Yankee blood
Oh do we remember

Those whose names we can't forget
We remember, we remember
Comrade spirits with us yet
Oh do we remember

Heartbreak Ridge and Pork Chop Hill
We remember, we remember
If we don't honor them who will
Oh do we remember

Those who died when far too young
We remember, we remember
It is for them this song is sung
Oh do we remember

Part 3
Echoes of Gratitude from Korea

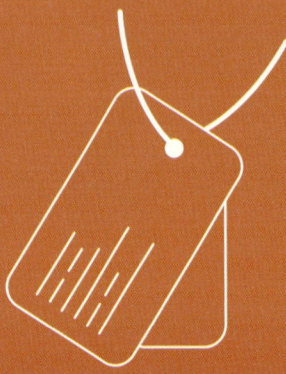

The Land Your Grandfather Visited	*Yoon Ha*
In the Names of Heroes	*Ph.D Hyuk Chul Kwon*
A Letter written in Love	*Minsub Kim*
Letter of Gratitude	*Jion Mun*
Ending Note	*Jihae Yun*

할아버지가 다녀가신 나라

세계인들의 아들 · 딸들이여!
고요한 나라에서 새벽에 전쟁이 났다.
도와주세요! 도와주세요!

세계 민주주의에 자유의 깃발이
펄럭이며 등에는 배낭, 철모를 쓰고
허리에 수통 차고, 가슴에 무전기
달랑거리며
달려온 파란 눈동자 그대여!
앞가슴 금빛 명찰이 찬란히 빛납니다.
감사합니다! 고맙습니다!

한국에 추운 겨울 나시고
세계사에도 없는 전쟁
피로 짓밟힌 자국위에
행진 행진 흘린 피 위에
우리나라는 우뚝 섰습니다.

그들의 친구들은 깊은 계곡 산비탈에서
철모를 쓰고 비스듬히 누워
사랑하는 부모 형제
이름을 부르며 아직도 그곳에
누워있습니다
아리랑 아리랑 노래를 부르며

The Land Your Grandfather Visited

Yoon Ha
President of the Angel Movement Foundation

Sons and daughters of the world,

In a quiet land, war broke out at dawn.

"Help us! Help us!"

The flag of freedom rose,

fluttering for the cause of world democracy.

With backpacks on your shoulders, helmets on your heads,

canteens at your sides, and radios dangling from your chests,

you blue-eyed souls came running.

The golden name tags on your uniforms shone brightly.

Thank you. Truly, thank you.

You endured the cold winters in Korea,

a war unlike any other in world history.

On blood-stained earth,

you marched and marched.

On the blood you shed, our nation rose again.

Your comrades lie still

on the slopes of deep valleys,

helmets slightly tilted,

calling out for beloved parents and siblings.

They remain there still,

singing softly—Arirang, Arirang.

할아버지께서 그리워했던 나라
이 나라는 미 브로드웨이처럼
찬란한 불빛이 반짝입니다.
할아버지께서 이름도 모르는 나라에
오셨고 그에 손주까지
3대가 찾아와 교육을 받고 함께하며

참전용사 22개국 1,957,733명,
전사 37,902명, 부상 103,450명
실종 3,950명, 포로 5,817명
그대들의 희생에 코리아는
우뚝 섰습니다.

고맙습니다. 감사합니다.
이 한마디로 갚을 수 없어
그들이 흘린 피 떠나가신 오솔길에
하얀 찔레꽃이 피었습니다.

매일 한 다발 꺾어 받쳐도 갚을 수 없는 은혜
참전용사 들이여! 그 후손들께도

용감한 할아버지의 옛이야기 들으시며
영원토록 세계로 미래로 세상 끝까지
빛나옵소서!

This land you dearly missed,

now sparkles with brilliant lights,

like Broadway in America.

To a land once unknown, you came.

And now, your grandchildren have come,

walking the same path,

three generations

learning, growing, and sharing life in Korea.

The twenty-two nations who came to help

1,957,733 brave souls they sent, 37,902 never returned

103,450 were wounded in battle, 3,950 still missing in the fog of war

5,817 were taken as prisoners.

Because of your sacrifice, Korea stands tall.

Thank you. Thank you.

Words are not enough

to repay the blood you shed.

Along the paths where you once walked,

white wild roses have now bloomed.

To the veterans and their descendants,

a single bouquet each day still falls short of the gratitude owed.

May your legacy shine forever

to the world, to the future,

to the ends of the earth.

영웅들의 이름으로

깊은 어둠이 한반도를 덮칠 때
당신들은 먼 이국 땅에서, 혹은 조국의 산과 들에서
총성과 포연 속에 한 줄기 희망이 되어
한국의 내일을 위해 일어섰습니다.

누군가는 이름도 남기지 못한 채
차가운 땅에 쓰러졌고
누군가는 총상과 상처를 안고
평생을 살아야 했으며
또 누군가는 전쟁의 기억 속에서
밤마다 깨어나야 했습니다.

그대들의 젊음은
피와 땀, 눈물로 얼룩졌으나
그 거룩한 희생과 용기가
오늘의 자유와 번영의 대한민국을 일구었습니다.

In the Names of Heroes

Ph.D Hyuk Chul Kwon
Director of North Korea Nuclear Research Institute

When deep darkness covered Korea,
you rose –from distant foreign shores,
from mountains and fields of your homeland,
becoming a ray of hope amid gunfire and smoke,
standing for Korea's tomorrow.

Some of you fell
without even a name to leave behind,
resting in the cold earth.
Some carried wounds and scars
that lasted a lifetime.
Others awoke each night,
haunted by the memories of war.

Your youth,
stained with blood, sweat, and tears,
became the sacred sacrifice and courage
that built today's free and prosperous Korea.

만약 그대들의 결의와 헌신이 없었다면
이 땅은 어둠에 묻혀
자유와 희망, 번영의 꿈은
영영 사라졌을 것입니다.

생존해 계신 용사들이여,
당신들의 삶과 이야기는
우리 모두의 가슴에 영원히 새겨질 것입니다.
전우를 잃은 슬픔,
몸과 마음의 상처,
그 모든 고통 위에 피어난
자유의 꽃을 우리는 결코 잊지 않겠습니다.

그대들의 이름을 부르며
깊은 감사와 존경을 바칩니다.
당신들의 희생 위에
오늘의 대한민국이 있습니다.

대한민국은 당신들의 용기와 희생을 영원히 기억할 것입니다.
감사합니다. 존경합니다.

Had it not been for your resolve and devotion,
this land would have been lost to darkness,
and the dream of freedom, hope, and prosperity would have vanished forever.

To the veterans who are still with us,
your lives and stories
will forever be engraved in our hearts.
The sorrow of fallen comrades,
the wounds on body and soul–
upon that pain
bloomed the flowers of freedom
that we will never forget.

We call out your names
with deepest gratitude and respect.
Upon your sacrifice
stands today's Republic of Korea.

Korea will remember your courage and sacrifice forever.
Thank you. We honor you.

감사의 편지

존경하는 UN 참전용사 여러분, 그리고 그 자녀와 가족 여러분께,

먼저 진심을 담아 깊은 감사의 인사를 전합니다.

1950년, 대한민국은 전례 없는 위기에 처해 있었습니다. 공산주의의 무력 침공으로 한반도는 순식간에 전쟁의 소용돌이에 휘말렸고, 나라의 존립마저 위협받던 그 순간, 여러분은 정의와 자유, 평화를 지키기 위한 신념으로 머나먼 이국 땅에 발을 내딛으셨습니다. 여러분의 숭고한 결단과 희생이 없었다면 오늘날 우리가 누리는 자유와 번영, 민주주의는 결코 존재하지 않았을 것입니다.

여러분의 후손들께도 깊이 감사드립니다. 당신들의 가족이 지킨 자유와 평화의 정신은 이 시대의 젊은이들에게도 큰 영감이 되고 있습니다. 여러분 역시 그 정신을 이어받은 자랑스러운 유산의 주인공이십니다. 대한민국은 이 은혜를 결코 잊지 않습니다.

여러분의 이름은 우리의 역사에, 교과서에, 추모비에, 그리고 우리의 마음 속에 영원히 기록되어 있습니다. 앞으로도 우리는 그 희생을 기억하며, 평화를 지키고 자유를 수호하는 책임 있는 국민으로 살아가겠습니다.

여러분과 여러분의 가족께 늘 건강과 평화, 그리고 존경이 함께하길 기원합니다.
진심을 담아 감사합니다.

A Letter written in Love

Minsub Kim
B.A. in Education, Seoul National University
Korean War Veteran Descendant

Dear UN Korean War Veterans, and Your Children and Families,
First and foremost, I extend my deepest and most sincere gratitude to all of you.

In 1950, the Republic of Korea faced an unprecedented crisis. With the sudden armed invasion by communist forces, the Korean Peninsula was quickly drawn into the vortex of war, and the very survival of our nation was at stake. At that critical moment, you set foot on a distant and unfamiliar land, guided by your firm belief in justice, freedom, and peace. Without your noble decision and sacrifice, the freedom, prosperity, and democracy we enjoy today would not have been possible.

I also express my deep appreciation to your descendants. The spirit of freedom and peace that your families defended continues to inspire today's younger generation. You are the proud heirs of that honorable legacy. The Republic of Korea will never forget your sacrifice.

Your names are forever engraved in our history books, in our classrooms, on memorials—and most importantly, in our hearts. We will continue to live as responsible citizens who honor your sacrifice, safeguard peace, and uphold freedom.

May health, peace, and honor always be with you and your families.
From the bottom of my heart, thank you.

감사의 편지

현재의 대한민국을 있게 해준 UN 참전용사분들 그리고 그 자녀와 가족 여러분께

안녕하십니까. 저는 육군사관학교 생도를 대표하여 이 글을 올립니다.
먼저, 조국의 자유와 평화를 지키기 위해 고귀한 희생과 헌신을 아끼지 않으신
여러분께 진심 어린 감사와 깊은 존경의 마음을 전합니다.

1950년 6월, 대한민국이 위태로웠던 그 때, 여러분들은 자신의 가족도, 고향도 뒤로한 채 이 땅을 위해 싸워주셨습니다. 전쟁의 두려움 속에서도 물러서지 않으셨고 끝내 자유와 평화를 지켜내신 그 희생과 헌신은 그 어떤 말로도 다 담을 수 없을만큼 깊고 값진 가치를 지니고 있습니다.
여러분의 헌신이 있었기에 오늘의 대한민국이 존재합니다. 그리고 그 정신은 저희가 이어가야 할 가장 고귀한 유산입니다. 저는 앞으로 어떠한 위기 속에서도 국민을 지키는 강인한 지휘관, 국가의 가치를 실현하는 책임 있는 군인이 될 것을 다짐합니다.
저는 대한민국을 위해 헌신하신 여러분의 뜻을 가슴 깊이 새기고,
장차 군을 이끌어갈 장교로서 국가와 국민을 지키기 위해 항상 최선을 다하는 군인이 되겠습니다. 여러분의 숭고한 희생과 정신을 늘 기억하고 계승해 나가겠습니다.

부디 건강하시고 여러분의 가정에 건강과 평화와 사랑이 가득하기를 기원합니다.
여러분이 지켜주신 이 나라를, 저희가 이어서 지켜나가겠습니다.
다시 한 번 감사드립니다.

Letter of Gratitude

Jion Mun
Korea Military Academy Cadet

Dear UN Veterans and your beloved families,

As the cadet representative of Korea Military Academy, I write this letter with deep respect and heartfelt gratitude.

More than seventy years ago, in June 1950, when the Republic of Korea was on the brink of collapse, you left behind your families and your homes to defend this country many of you had never seen before. In the face of fear, pain, and unimaginable hardship, you stood firm. Your courage and sacrifice laid the foundation for the peace and freedom we enjoy today. No words can truly express the depth of your sacrifice and dedication.

Because of your selfless devotion, the Republic of Korea has grown into a thriving democracy—a country that remembers its past and works toward a better future. Your bravery and values remain a guiding light for our generation. You have given us more than just safety—you have given us hope, dignity, and the responsibility to honor your legacy.

As a cadet and future leader of the Armed Forces, I will hold your sacrifice close to my heart. I will strive to live with the same sense of duty and compassion that you showed. Your story will not be forgotten.

We will remember, we will honor, and we will carry forward the spirit you have passed down to us. May you and your families be blessed with lasting health, peace, and love. Thank you truly for everything. With deepest respect and gratitude.

Ending Note

My name is Jihae Yun, and I had the profound honor of serving as the editor of this book.

I extend my deepest gratitude to the 22 descendants of the Korean War veterans who contributed their stories to this publication. This book could not have come to life without your time and the depth of emotion you so generously shared. I also offer my sincere thanks and respect to all of the veterans, including the grandfathers remembered in these pages, whose courage and sacrifice have given us the peace and freedom we cherish today.

This project held deep personal significance for me. Both my paternal and maternal grandfathers served in the Korean War. My grandfather on my father's side fought as a student soldier while still in high school and my grandfather on my mother's side served on the front lines. I grew up listening to my grandfather's stories of the war, and as I matured, I came to understand the long-term emotional and psychological burdens my other grandfather carried in silence. Their legacies have lived on in my heart, and working on this book became a way for me to honor them and so many others like them.

As I read through each of the 22 stories—one by one, line by line—I often found

Jihae Yun
University of Toronto, Trinity College
Korean War Veteran Descendant

myself in tears. These were not just accounts of history, but deeply human stories of young men who left behind their homes and families to fight for the freedom of a distant land. Many were barely adults, yet they chose compassion over comfort, sacrifice over safety. Their bravery, especially for the sake of innocent children and civilians, moved me beyond words.

Among many unforgettable quotes, a few resonated deeply within me:

From Canada:

"Although riddled with PTSD, he once told me that even knowing everything that had happened, the trepidations, anxieties, and fears that were faced, I would do it all over again without question."

From New Zealand:

"Many good men died for a good cause, and every time I see Korea's progress, I feel proud."

From Türkiye:

"Son, why do you want to go to Korea?" "For the innocent children…"

"Ahmet Şahna and countless other unsung heroes were not just soldiers carrying weapons; they were compassionate and courageous individuals who upheld their humanity even in the darkest times."

These words reminded me of the nobility of human compassion. They taught me that the Korean War was not only a battle for land or ideology, but a testament to the boundless power of selfless love.

The Republic of Korea has achieved extraordinary progress in the decades since the war—growth that is nothing short of miraculous. This nation stands on the grace of God and on the blood, sweat, and sacrifice of our ancestors, both Korean and from across the world. At the heart of it all was love: love for the innocent children, love for fellow soldiers, and love for a nation they embraced as their own.

I pray that Korea will continue to grow as a nation that serves with love and humility. I believe this begins with myself, with my family, my school, my workplace, and our nation, and that from here, a ripple of good influence will reach the world.

May Korea broaden its vision and become a guiding light of integrity and compassion to the world. This, I believe, is the sacred responsibility entrusted to us and to the generations that follow.

In Korea's most painful and difficult times, there were those who did not turn away from our suffering but instead loved their neighbors, some even giving their lives. I pray that this missionary spirit will take deep root in the soul of our nation, so that Korea may bear abundant fruit of love and service that are pleasing to God.

This book has been the product of many long days and late nights—writing, revising, editing, reaching out to contributors, and preparing for publication both online and in-person. It wasn't an easy journey as it demanded my whole heart with countless hours of dedication. That is why, if even one reader picks up this book and feels a deeper gratitude toward those who fought for Korea, or dares to imagine a greater future for our country, then every ounce of effort has been worthwhile.

To all of the Korean War veterans and beloved families,
from the bottom of my heart, I want to say thank you. Korea will always remember you.

THE STORY OF
UN KOREAN WAR VETERANS

EDITOR	Ha Young Shin
ASSOCIATE EDITOR	Jihae Yun
SUPERVISION	Hosub Shim
EDITORIAL DESIGN	JiHyun Im
PUBLISHER	KORAD
E-MAIL	hyshinkk@hanmail.net
PHONE	+82-02-2266-0751
PRICE	15,000 KRW
ISBN	979-11-89931-92-6 (03340)

©2025, KORAD

This publication has been issued under an agreement with the copyright holder, KORAD. Therefore, any use of this work, in whole or in part, requires prior consent from KORAD.

This book includes original manuscripts, testimonies, and materials submitted by individuals from various countries. These contents remain the intellectual property of the respective contributors and have been included with their prior written permission. The views and opinions expressed in the essays are those of the individual authors and do not necessarily reflect those of the editor or publisher.

Certain photographs and reference materials were provided by third-party contributors. Every effort has been made to ensure appropriate usage and proper attribution. However, some materials may be subject to third-party copyright. Should any rights holder raise a concern, the publisher is committed to resolving the matter promptly and appropriately.